Young Readers Edition

THE

AN INNOCENT MAN,

SUN

A WRONGFUL CONVICTION,

DOES

AND THE LONG PATH TO JUSTICE

SHINE

Anthony Ray Hinton

with Lara Love Hardin and
Olugbemisola Rhuday-Perkovich

SQUARE
FISH

FEIWEL AND FRIENDS · NEW YORK

SQUARE FISH

An imprint of Macmillan Publishing Group, LLC
120 Broadway, New York, NY 10271 • mackids.com

Copyright © 2022 by Anthony Ray Hinton and
Olugbemisola Rhuday-Perkovich.
All rights reserved.

Square Fish and the Square Fish logo are trademarks of Macmillan
and are used by Feiwel and Friends under license from Macmillan.

Our books may be purchased in bulk for promotional, educational, or
business use. Please contact your local bookseller or the Macmillan
Corporate and Premium Sales Department at (800) 221-7945 ext. 5442
or by email at MacmillanSpecialMarkets@macmillan.com.

Library of Congress Control Number 2022901734

Originally published in the United States by Feiwel and Friends
First Square Fish edition, 2024
Book designed by Trisha Previte
Square Fish logo designed by Filomena Tuosto
Printed in the United States of America by Berryville Graphics,
Martinsburg, West Virginia

ISBN 978-1-250-32711-6
10 9 8 7 6 5 4 3 2 1

AR: 5.7 / LEXILE: 810L

*For Lester Bailey, because the friends we make
when we are kids can be our best friends for life*

FOREWORD

On April 3, 2015, Anthony Ray Hinton was released from prison after facing execution for nearly thirty years on Alabama's death row for a crime he did not commit. Mr. Hinton is one of the longest-serving condemned prisoners facing execution in America to be proved innocent and then released.

Thirty years is a long time to be held in solitary confinement, condemned for something you didn't do. It is unjust and tragic, but it happens in America too often. It's one of the reasons some of us believe we need to improve our system and eliminate the bias and unfair practices that made it far too easy for Mr. Hinton to be wrongly condemned.

Mr. Hinton grew up poor and Black in rural Alabama. He learned to be a keen and thoughtful observer of the harsh realities of Jim Crow segregation and the way racial bias constrained the lives of people of color. He was taught by his remarkable mother to never see race or judge people because of their color. He was a poor man in a criminal justice system that treats you better if you are rich and guilty than if you are poor and innocent.

He is blessed with an extraordinary sense of humor, which he relies on to overcome the racial barriers that condemn so many. He lived with his mother until he was in his late twenties and worked as a contract laborer. He had never been accused of a violent act before his arrest.

One night while he was locked in a supermarket warehouse

cleaning floors in Bessemer, Alabama, a restaurant manager fifteen miles away was abducted, robbed, and shot by a single gunman as he left work. The victim survived and later misidentified Mr. Hinton as the person who'd robbed him. Despite the fact that Mr. Hinton was working in a secure facility with a guard who recorded everyone's arrival and departure, miles from the crime scene, police went to the home of Mr. Hinton's mother, where they retrieved an old .38 caliber pistol. Alabama state forensic workers asserted that this recovered gun was not only the one used in this recent robbery and attempted murder but also in two other murders in the Bessemer area where restaurant managers had been robbed and killed at closing. Based on this gun evidence, Mr. Hinton was arrested and indicted for both murders, and State prosecutors announced they would seek the death penalty. Mr. Hinton passed a polygraph examination administered by police that confirmed his innocence, but State officials ignored this information and his alibi and persisted in obtaining two convictions and death sentences.

At trial, Mr. Hinton's appointed lawyer failed to obtain a competent expert to rebut the State's false claims about his mother's gun. For fourteen years, he could not obtain the legal help he needed to prove his innocence. I met Mr. Hinton in 1999, and he made quite an impression. He was thoughtful, sincere, genuine, compassionate, and funny, so it was easy to want to help Anthony Ray Hinton, although it was worrisome to think how difficult it might prove to win his freedom.

I worked with my staff at the Equal Justice Initiative to engage three of the nation's top firearms examiners, who all testified that the gun obtained from Mr. Hinton's mother could not be matched to the crime evidence. It took fourteen more years of contested litigation and a rare unanimous ruling from the U.S. Supreme Court before Mr. Hinton was released in 2015. During his time on Alabama's death row, Mr. Hinton watched fifty-four men walk past his door on their way to be executed. The execution chamber was thirty feet from his cell.

Mr. Hinton was sustained during his long years on Alabama's death row by a childhood friend who never failed to visit him over the course of nearly thirty years. Lester Bailey insisted that Mr. Hinton never feel alone or abandoned. Mr. Hinton learned to engage those around him and create an identity on death row unlike anything I've ever seen. Not only did he shape the lives of dozens of other death row prisoners but also those of correctional officers who sought Mr. Hinton's advice and counsel on everything from marriage and faith to the struggles of day-to-day life.

While his case created years of disappointment and frustration for Mr. Hinton and cost me many sleepless nights after each adverse legal ruling, we both could be frequently seen doubled over with laughter in the visitation room at Holman State Prison. Such is the extraordinary power of Ray (as his friends call him) Hinton and his remarkable spirit.

I've visited countless prisons and jails to see hundreds of clients during the course of my career. I'm usually ignored or merely tolerated by correctional staff during these visits. There have been times when I have been harassed or challenged by prison staff who seem to resent incarcerated people getting legal visits. Visiting Ray Hinton was unlike any other legal visit for me. Never have more guards, correctional staff, and prison workers pulled me aside to offer assistance or question me about how they could help than during the many years I have worked with Ray. I have never experienced anything like it.

I have represented scores of condemned prisoners during my thirty years of law practice. Many of my clients were innocent people wrongly convicted or condemned. However, no one I have represented has inspired me more than Anthony Ray Hinton, and I believe his compelling and unique story will similarly inspire our nation and readers all over the world.

Reading his story is difficult but necessary. We need to learn things about our criminal legal system, about the legacy of racial bias in America and the way it can blind us to just and fair treatment of people. We need to understand the dangers posed by the politics of fear and anger that can cause us to accept things we should never accept, tolerate things we should never tolerate. We also need to learn about human dignity, about human worth and value. We need to think about the fact that we are all more than the worst thing we have done. Anthony Ray Hinton's story helps us understand some of these problems and ultimately what it means to survive, to overcome, and to forgive.

Every person who reads this story has the power to make a difference in the world, to reject unjust and unfair treatment of other people. I believe we all have an obligation to do so. No one should ever go through what Mr. Hinton went through in America, but it will happen again unless we educate ourselves, insist on greater reliability and fairness in our criminal justice system, care more about the poor and those who are vulnerable, and pay attention to how our local systems of justice work.

Mr. Hinton's story is one of forgiveness, friendship, and

triumph. This book is something of a miracle, because there were many moments when I believe both of us feared he would never survive to tell his story. We should be grateful that he did survive, because his witness, his life, and his journey together create an unforgettable inspiration.

Bryan Stevenson, attorney

PROLOGUE:
PURE EVIL

"More so than the evidence, I have never had as strong a feeling in trying any other case that the defendant just radiated guilt and pure evil as much as in the Hinton trial."

—Prosecutor Bob McGregor

Ray had often heard of people pinpointing the exact moment that their lives had "changed forever." But what did that really mean? How could anyone really know when their life changed . . . *forever*? And could anyone ever see it coming? When had it happened for him?

The day he was arrested for murder?

Or had it happened before that, in tiny ways, day by day, without him even realizing that bad luck and a few mistakes had brought him to a cell the size of a bathroom?

Maybe what he did didn't matter, maybe the choices he made didn't count—when you were born Black and poor in the South that still was so often on the wrong side of civil rights, maybe then it meant that men like Anthony Ray Hinton would have always ended up right where he was.

It was hard to know.

But Ray had plenty of time to think about it, living his entire life in a room five feet wide by seven feet long—oh yeah, he had plenty of time to think about what could have been, what he could have done, what he could never be. Just like anyone else, Ray had grown up with dreams. A baseball scholarship, maybe marriage and kids. A fancy job, a nice car. He had dreamed of so much, but nothing like this nightmare he was living.

The thing was, he'd been a pretty good guy. He'd always believed that if you did the right thing and lived a decent life, you'd be okay. But now he knew that pain and tragedy and injustice happen—to anyone, even the good guys. And when he thought back on the horrors he'd lived through, Ray wanted so much to believe that what mattered most was how you chose to live after the pain, after the tragedy. That was when you could choose to change your life forever.

But still, he wondered: Did it matter at all? Did he?

Chapter One

BENT BUT NOT BROKEN

"The situation in Alabama and Mississippi which is spectacular and surprises the country is nationwide . . . Because until today, all the Negroes in this country in one way or another, in different fashions, North and South, are kept in what is, in effect, prison. In the North, one lives in ghettos and in the South, the situation is so intolerable as to become sinister not only for Mississippi or Alabama or Florida but for the whole future of this country."

—James Baldwin[1]

"I am in Birmingham because injustice is here . . . Birmingham is probably the most thoroughly segregated city in the United States. Its ugly record of brutality is widely known."

—Rev. Dr. Martin Luther King, Jr., *Letter from Birmingham Jail*

WEST JEFFERSON HIGH SCHOOL, MAY 1974

They may beat you now and then," Ray's mom used to tell him, "but that don't mean they have to break you. You don't change who you are and how you was raised for anyone.

---

1 www.youtube.com/watch?v=FpRziHGxeEU
www.pbs.org/wnet/americanmasters/6-james-baldwin-quotes-race/15142/

And I didn't raise no child to have a tantrum in the middle of a baseball field or anywhere."

So even though the May Alabama sun felt like it was burning a hole in his helmet, even though Ray knew this pitcher was a sore loser who would throw his glove, his hat, even kick the fence in the kind of display of poor sportsmanship that Ray couldn't even let himself think of—even though this guy had just thrown an out-of-control curveball that just barely landed into the catcher's glove far outside of the plate, and the umpire had had the nerve to call it a strike, his laughter daring Ray to lose his cool . . . even with all of that, Ray just stared the pitcher down and let the catcher's and umpire's snide whispers roll off his back.

Because Ray was more afraid to let his mom down than he was of these white boys, or the sea of white faces in the stands. He was no stranger to hostile stares and hearing the n-word muttered in disgust when he walked by. After four years of being bused to a white school, he knew his mom's words by heart. "You study. You keep your head down. You keep your eyes down. And when the teachers talk to you, be polite and follow the rules. You go to school, and then you get home. Fast."

It was more than just advice. It felt like a matter of life and death, and in Birmingham, Alabama, in 1974, it was. When you played sports after school, there was no bus to take you home. And if you were a Black child, you didn't risk walking home alone. Ray's best friend, Lester, would wait for him, somewhere out of sight so that he wouldn't attract attention, and they'd make the long trip home together—they were like brothers, and stuck together like glue even though Ray was older by two years. It hadn't always been that way. When Ray was six, he didn't think he'd have much use for a four-year-old best friend. But one day Ray got in trouble with his mom, and as punishment, he had to sit in a chair, inside, for hours, while it seemed like the whole world was outside playing and enjoying a beautiful day. And then little Lester came and sat beside him. They didn't talk (they couldn't risk it, not during a punishment); Ray just sat, enduring his consequences, and Lester sat right there beside him. And sat, and sat. Lester stayed with Ray for hours, until the last shouts of joyful play rang out, until it was time for everyone to go inside. That was the day Ray realized he had a friend for life. The kind of friend who'd skip fun in the sunshine to stay by his side for as long as Ray needed him, no matter what.

Now in high school, they still stuck together, and the stakes were even higher. Ray and Lester were always ready to defend themselves or take cover on the long walk home from these baseball games. It wasn't a leisurely walk, or a playful one. This was about getting home alive. Sometimes it seemed like a horror movie, or a war zone. That was Ray's real life, now that integration was the law of the land.

But the game wasn't over yet. Ray stared straight ahead and waited for the next pitch. He'd be ready, whatever it was. Rumor had it that there were scouts at this game. He was a power hitter, and he dreamed of winning a baseball scholarship that took him far, far away from Birmingham. His nine older siblings had escaped; "Bombingham" was a place of horrors for Black people like him, including Martin Luther King, Jr., and the thousands of children who'd been thrown in jail for the crime of asking to be recognized as human; the people who were reminded every time they sat at a lunch counter for a burger

3

and a milkshake that they were not at all welcome, and only being served because it was the law; the four little girls who had been killed in a church bombing when they were doing nothing but living in their brown skin. 1974 Birmingham didn't feel that different from 1964, or 1954.

Even so, in his all-Black community, Ray felt safe. The people looked out for each other. If someone got in trouble three streets away, their mom would know about it before they could even get home to tell her. They were poor, and segregated, but there was love. Everyone was family.

Then Ray left the safety of his all-Black school for the integrated West Jefferson High, where he got another kind of traumatic education every day, one filled with as much hate and racist injustice as it was filled with math and English.

Once during basketball season, Ray scored thirty points in the first half of a game—an away game at that. Thirty points! It was a record for his school. He walked off the court to the sound of the crowd chanting his name. "Hin-ton! Hin-ton! Hin-ton!" Even the fans of the opposing team were doing it. Ray was so proud. But none of Ray's teammates were smiling or high-fiving him, and Ray couldn't understand why.

Then his coach went to center court and started yelling at the crowd, trying to shut them up.

"What are they saying?" Ray asked one of his teammates, who just shook his head. "What are they saying?"

Then his teammate told him. They weren't chanting his name. They were shouting the n-word, over and over. Even when they didn't beat you, they tried to break you.

But Ray wasn't having it. He had the best batting average in Birmingham, maybe even in the whole state of Alabama, so he dreamed of miracles. Hank Aaron was from Alabama. So was Willie Mays. Maybe one day a little boy would dream of hitting home runs like him, Anthony Ray Hinton. Maybe one day he would be someone's hero.

The pitcher spit and did his windup dance. Curveball, fastball, knuckleball—it didn't matter what was coming because Ray was ready for it. He'd been playing street ball with an old broom handle and a homemade ball for as long as he could remember. In street ball, you swung at the pitch you were given, and you made the best of it. He planted his feet, and . . .

"That's my baby!" Ray heard his mom's proud shout and turned to see her standing by the chain link fence next to the bleachers. She didn't have a car; the money she made cleaning houses was barely enough to keep a roof over their heads ever since an accident in the coal mine had put Ray's father in an institution. How had she gotten all the way to his game?

She waved a white handkerchief and yelled again.

"Go, baby! That's my baby!" Ray weighed 230 pounds and towered over her, but he was her baby, no matter what.

And Ray was going to make her proud.

He watched the ball come closer and closer, like it was in slow motion, like it was just him and the ball—no cheating ump or sneering catcher, no angry white faces in the stands.

He dropped the bat and hit the ground hard. WHOOSH! The pitcher had aimed right at his head! Would the ump call this a strike too?

"Ball!" called the ump. The pitcher, watching Ray wince with pain as he picked up the bat and got ready again, smirked. Ray didn't care. This guy was going to hit Ray, or Ray was going to hit the ball—nothing was going to stop Ray from getting on base.

The next pitch zoomed out of the pitcher's glove—a change-up, the kind of pitch that sent a lot of players swinging into a complete circle, looking silly and dazed. Ray watched the ball fly toward him, he watched and waited and waited and watched—and then he swung. He swung for his team, for his mama, and for Lester. He swung for every kid in his neighborhood who was going to be called a nasty, hate-filled name that day.

And when Ray's bat met that ball, he heard the sweet and sharp sound, like thunder on a hot day in August, of the ball hitting the bat exactly where you want it.

He dropped the bat and ran.

"That's my baby! That's my baby!"

He rounded first, and out of the corner of his eye, Ray saw his mom waving her arms in the air. On his way to second, he looked up as the ball soared up, up, and out over the center-field fence. Then he knew he didn't need to run anymore. He heard the shortstop mutter something as he rounded to third, but whatever it was, Ray didn't care. He kept going, enjoying every moment of his home run.

When he crossed home plate, Ray looked over to see the pitcher throw his glove in the dirt, and that made Ray smile wide. *They can beat you, but they can't break you.* Looked like the pitcher's mama hadn't taught him the same things Ray's mama had. But then again, maybe she didn't need to.

Ray went on to hit a triple and another home run; his team won the game, 7–2. There was a scout there, but he didn't ask to speak to Ray. Ray's mom had had to leave early, and after the game Ray and Lester started their one-and-a-half-hour walk home on a two-lane road. They didn't talk much, because they had to stay alert. Lester watched ahead, Ray looked behind so that they could see any car that was coming even before they could hear it. If it was someone they knew, Ray could catch a ride home to his mom's home-cooked dinner. If it was a car they didn't recognize, they'd jump into the ditch at the side of the road and hide the best they could.

As an unfamiliar car sent them scrambling into the ditch for the second time, Ray looked up at the sky. He could get angry or he could have some faith. He had a choice, and right there in that ditch, hiding from the real possibility of white violence, Ray chose to love every single shade of blue that the sky wanted to show him. And when he turned his head to the right, he could see what looked like ten different shades of green. There was beauty if he looked for it. The dirt smelled a little bit like burned sugar. His mom was waiting at home with some grits and turkey neck and a sweet piece of cobbler. He had just played a great baseball game, and even if the scouts and the coaches and the colleges didn't want to pay attention, Ray knew he could hit like nobody else. He had his best friend at his side. Things could have been worse. They could always be worse.

As they waited for the car to pass, Ray listened to his own breathing, listened to Lester breathing right beside him. He wanted to protect Lester, his mom, his sisters and brothers—everyone in the whole world who couldn't walk down a street without feeling some kind of fear just because of the color of their skin.

Ray didn't ever want to get used to this.

He didn't want this to ever be normal.

The car passed; they were safe—for now.

"Let's get going," he said, and they climbed out of the ditch and continued their long walk home.

Chapter Two

FREEDOM MATTERS

"If you are big and brave enough to throw a rock, you'd better be big and brave enough not to hide your hands behind your back when you get caught. You show your hands, and you own up to what you done."

—Buhlar Hinton

MARY LEE MINE NO. 2, 1975

Ray had never really believed he would end up working the coal mines, but there weren't many options for a young Black man after high school graduation. No scholarship. No college. He didn't even have the extra ten dollars to buy his class ring. The coal mines were the only place he could get a decent wage right out of high school, and he couldn't afford to turn his back on a steady job. He had an "in"—his dad had worked the mines before him, and others put in a good word for him. Ray was known to be easygoing, likable. He didn't have a reputation as a troublemaker or "problem." Some men might have said they would kill for the opportunity for a decent job in the mines, even though it was a place where they could easily die. It was dangerous work, as Ray already knew. His father had literally been knocked senseless in a mining accident, and a loose boulder or razor-sharp sliver of shale could mean the end for a miner. Ray worked in small shafts and tunnels where he had less than four feet of height to maneuver in. He spent endless hours in dark, dank air, in a world with no light and no color. It was dark when he went down in the morning, it was dark all day, and it was dark when he got outside at night. He struggled with the heavy machinery; his work had to be done right or men would die. Some days it felt like the best Ray could do was pray that the roof's weight held.

He hated every second of it.

He wasn't meant to be kept in a small space; he didn't like to be hunched over, to feel like walls were slowly closing in on him and there was no place to run, no place where there was light and air and space for a man to breathe. Ray felt like he was climbing into his own coffin every day. He let his imagination take him out of there, to the wide-open western skies, or up to Maine to eat lobster, to Mexico, or the warm, blue waters of Key West, Florida. In his mind, he would travel anywhere but into that black, dark pit where every breath was full of float dust that brought coal and rock and dirt into his lungs, where it settled in and took root as if to punish you for disturbing it in the first place.

Ray had grown up with old men who hadn't gone into the mines in twenty years but their handkerchiefs still turned black every time they coughed or blew their noses or wiped their foreheads on a hot summer day. He saw other men dying before they even got a chance to retire—watched them struggling to breathe from lungs that were full of a sickness that didn't have a name. Ray didn't want to die in the mine or sweat coal for the rest of his life or have the mine grow in his lungs until it choked everything out, but what else was a guy to do when he was ready to work and earn his way in the world? The sad truth was, the best way to go up in the world was to go down into the mines. And the more dangerous the job, the better it paid.

But bad as it was, Ray's time in the mines didn't even end with the accident that left him with a concussion and his nose almost completely sliced off. Even after the twenty-two stitches, Ray spent another five years in the mines. He kept going back.

Until he couldn't anymore.

One day, he woke up late and the sun was shining and he could hear birds chirping and the sky was the brightest blue he had ever seen. Ray just knew he couldn't go down in that dark place again. He wanted to be in the sunshine. Lester worked at a different mine, and he had no plans of giving up a solid job anytime soon. He just shook his head when Ray told him he'd rather be poor in the light than rich in the dark. Ray dreamed of big adventures and a life where a man could be rewarded for his hard work without putting his life at risk. He imagined going to law school or even business school. He'd be a silk-suited CEO or lawyer, out-arguing anyone in a courtroom, or maybe a doctor or firefighter. At twenty-four, he'd stopped dreaming of baseball—that hurt too much. He knew that if he had been born someone else, he would have gotten a scholarship and gone to college, maybe even been drafted, and that knowledge hurt so much he put that dream away.

Ray also put away any hope of rides with neighbors to and from work.

He and his mom had been forced to move out of Praco; they loaded their house on the back of a truck and moved it to a piece of land in Burnwell, a short ways away from Praco. Ray was the youngest child and the one who was expected to stay with his mom and help her out. All but two of his siblings had left Alabama altogether. It wasn't an easy place to live. But staying with his mom was a joy for Ray. He loved her more than anything. Her happiness was his happiness, and the other way around, and as far as Ray was concerned, that was the way it had always been and would always be. (Of course, he also didn't mind her cooking for him. She would cook for him anytime day or night, and to Ray, that food tasted just like love felt.)

But now in his new neighborhood, Ray needed a car more than ever. He had gone from hiding in ditches away from strange cars on the road to getting into strange cars because he was desperate for a ride. It was a risk, because it wasn't like the world had gotten any safer for a Black man.

Ray couldn't get a job without a car, and he couldn't buy a car without a job, so he was stuck, and sick of it. He was so tired of being without, of wanting, of struggling to make a dollar outside of the mine. Ray had always been a hard worker, but even he couldn't walk ten or fifteen miles to a job and then back home again. Something had to give.

That something gave on a Saturday. Ray woke up, put on his best church clothes, had breakfast with his mom, kissed her goodbye, and then caught a ride from a friend of his. Ray asked to be dropped off a few blocks away from a car lot he had seen before. It was like he was looking at himself doing something—like watching a movie. Some days Ray wanted to be somebody else so much, it was like he really believed he was that imaginary person. And on that Saturday, Ray wasn't a poor kid who was struggling to keep a job—he was a guy just out of college who had landed a great corporate position and was shopping for a brand-new car. He walked up and down the rows of cars, and a shiny, sky-blue Cutlass Supreme caught his eye. The blue velvet seats were so soft they felt like clouds, and its four headlights made it look like the car had a face, and that face was smiling just for Ray.

"You want to take her for a test drive?" asked the salesman.

Ray nodded. "I'd like that. I'd like to see how she drives."

And just like that, the salesman handed over the keys. "These belong to you."

Inside the car, Ray breathed deeply. It smelled like Christmas morning, and Easter Sunday, and Thanksgiving dinner, and his birthday all rolled into one.

He drove out of the lot, feeling strong and powerful and like there was nothing in this world he couldn't do. He got on the highway, pressed his foot down on the gas pedal, and listened to the engine roar. He drove for over an hour, and when he turned around and headed back toward Birmingham, it was easy to pass the exit that led to the car lot and instead head back toward his mama's house.

He never went back to the lot. Just then, Ray felt a hope so big he thought his heart might jump right out of his chest. Ray couldn't wait to show his mama his new car. He couldn't wait to tell her that life was really going to be changing for them both. This car was his. "These belong to you," the salesman had said. It felt so real.

Ray held on to that car for two years, kept it in pristine condition. His mom was happy he could drive her to the store and run errands. She always sat straight up in that car, with a big smile on her face. She trusted Ray, and that gnawed at him every time he drove with her at his side. What if they got into an accident, or had a breakdown, and the police came? What would his mom think of what he'd done? He wanted to return the car, but what would he tell his mother when it was suddenly gone?

He was trapped in a lie that had grown so big he couldn't find his way out of it.

The guilt felt like it was rotting him from the inside out.

He'd never been more scared to tell anyone anything, but there was no avoiding it.

"I need to tell you something. Something serious."

His mom was washing dishes, and she turned off the sink and dried her hands on a dish towel. "Well, let's have a sit now. You don't talk about something serious standing up."

She got out two glasses and a pitcher of sweet tea out of the fridge.

"And you never talk about something serious without having a drink," she added. She poured the tea and sat next to Ray at the kitchen table. "Now, what's all this fuss about?"

"I did something. I did something wrong."

She looked in Ray's eyes and took a sip of tea. She didn't say anything. His mom could say more in silence than most people could say in a ten-minute speech. She waited. Sipped more tea. Then she nodded at Ray, and the whole story came out. He told her about the test drive and the wanting to be someone else, someone different. He told her that he had never paid for that car and now everything was crashing down and he didn't know what to do next.

Ray's mom looked at him with the saddest eyes he had ever seen. "Are you sorry?"

"Yes."

"Are you going to make it right?"

"Yes, ma'am."

"Well, then, you go make it right. You go to the police station, and you tell them everything, and you face the music. I didn't raise you to take something that don't belong to you, but I did raise you to admit your wrongs. You aren't a boy anymore, and I can't protect you from this. You admit what you did to them police, and then you admit what you did to God. He will forgive you, and so will I. But you need to choose who you are, Ray. You need to choose what sort of man you are going to be. You need to choose now. I know you will choose right. I know you will." Her eyes were so sad, and Ray vowed right then and there that he would never, ever do anything to put that look of hurt in his mama's eyes again. He would make her proud.

Ray called a friend to drive him to the police station, where he confessed. He ended up having to spend only a few months in a work release program. He went to Kilby Prison just to be processed, but was only there long enough for them to get his name into the system.

That was definitely long enough. There was nothing glamorous about prison. The food was horrible. The smell was horrible. The lack of freedom made every cell in his body ache. No car, no money, no job, nothing was ever worth risking his freedom for. At night, away from home, he spent a lot of time thinking about who and what mattered in this life.

God mattered. Lester mattered.

His freedom mattered.

And most of all, his mom mattered.

Ray had to serve a year and a half on parole, out of prison but supervised and monitored, but he didn't care. He could have been on parole for fifty years—he knew he would never, ever do anything that was outside the law again.

"As God is my witness," Ray said to Lester, "I will never take something that doesn't belong to me again."

Chapter Three

THAT'S MY BABY

"What is one thing you wish you could say to young Ray after his death sentence was handed down?"

"I would tell him that hope is a choice, and to pace himself. I don't think I would tell him that it was going to take thirty years for the truth to be known."

—Anthony Ray Hinton

FEBRUARY 1985

On February 23, 1985, someone robbed Mrs. Winner's Chicken & Biscuits restaurant, stole $2,200, and killed the manager, John Davidson. Someone took a son away from his parents and a husband away from his wife. There were no fingerprints. No eyewitnesses. No DNA. Anyone could have done it.

Somebody got away with murder.

JULY 1985

By the summer of 1985, Ray knew that he couldn't go on working at The Brass Works any longer. Always having to work on Saturdays was taking a toll. After five days at work, Saturdays were for potlucks at church, barbecues with friends, running errands with his mom or taking her fishing, and college football. His church was always looking for men on Saturdays to help with car washes and building repairs, and Ray hated that he couldn't help his church family.

Monday through Friday, Ray worked as hard as he could—always showed up on time and gave it his best—but come Saturday, it was like a switch flipped, and he knew he wasn't doing his employer justice. Eventually, he left, with no hard feelings.

Ray had just turned twenty-nine, and he still didn't know what he wanted to be when he grew up. He knew he didn't want to be a coal miner. He definitely knew he didn't want to be in prison. He wasn't cut out to be a deckhand on a tug hauling coal up and down the river.

Ray just wanted to make a living, pay his bills, buy a nice car, get married, and have children. (He was hoping that future wife would be willing to live at his mama's house; he wouldn't leave his mom on her own.) Ray's mother never once rushed him to figure things out. She just loved him absolutely and unconditionally, the way she always did.

In the meantime, Ray made plans to work for a company called Manpower, which provided temporary labor to businesses around Birmingham. Manpower wasn't going to be a whole lot of money, but it was something, and he was optimistic that moving from business to business and doing different jobs would help him learn what it was he wanted to do with his life. Ray had been out of high school ten years, but he still loved to learn new things, to talk to new people, and go to new places. He thought about opening up a restaurant where he could serve people the food his mama had been making for so long—she'd taught Ray to cook everything she made him.

Her cooking lessons always began with, "If it makes you happy, you'd better be able to make it yourself. I don't see no wife on your arm anytime soon."

Ray's mama always had a way of getting her point across.

Ray and his family celebrated the Fourth of July in 1985 like they did every year—an endless supply of mouth-watering barbecue, friends from church, and sweet tea by the gallon. There was no bigger holiday in Alabama than the Fourth. Fireworks, watermelon, gunnysack races, egg tosses, and kids running around while grown-ups squirted them with water from a hose. Black people and white people may have been separate throughout the year, but something about the Fourth brought neighborhoods and people together like nothing else. To Ray it felt like the one time of year it seemed like all of Birmingham fell in love with each other.

This Fourth, Ray's mom wore her best white hat and her blue dress with red piping at the sleeves. Ray watched her laugh with the ladies from church and felt a joy so big he couldn't even contain it. In just a few weeks, he would be off parole, and all those mistakes from his past would be put to rest. He had a new girlfriend, and he was hopeful that his start at Manpower the next day would lead to something bigger.

Ray turned to Lester and said, "This holiday feels just like the Pledge of Allegiance."

"Man, what do you mean?"

"You know, one nation under God with liberty and justice for all. Everything today feels like that. Hopeful. Like justice and freedom and anything is possible. You know?"

"I guess so. It kind of just feels like another hot Fourth of July, but I see what you mean."

Ray felt such a love for Lester and for his mom in her dress and hat and for Alabama and for hot days in July with sweet tea that cools you from the inside out that he was actually at a loss for words.

Then he swallowed a lump in his throat that had come up out of nowhere. "Just feels like change is in the air," Ray said. "I don't know." Lester looked up at an overcast sky and laughed.

"Feels like thunder to me."

● ● ●

Ray's mom had asked him to cut the front lawn, but all Ray wanted to do was drink something cool in the shade of his mama's living room.

"I'll cut that grass tomorrow," he said, settling down on the couch.

She looked at him in that quiet way she had that meant business. "Now, I'm trying my best to see how you get to 'I'll cut it tomorrow' from my telling you to cut it now."

Ray and his siblings had grown up knowing that once they were told to do something, they rarely got out of doing it. But if anyone had a chance of sweet-talking their mama, it was Ray.

Not today.

A few moments later, Ray cranked up the old lawn mower and started running through Bible verses in his head. He had to pick something to recite later that day at church, and he wanted to look good for both God and his girlfriend. As he went back and forth across the front lawn, he finally settled on one that seemed perfect for the day—Philippians 2:14–15. He knew it would make his mama smile to hear him read the beginning of the verse: "Do all things without grumbling or disputing."

Suddenly, Ray looked up and saw two white men standing on the back porch. They were staring at him, and neither was smiling. He cut off the lawn mower as the rest of the verse ran through his mind: "So that you will prove yourselves to be blameless and innocent children of God, above reproach in the midst of a crooked and perverse generation, among whom you appear as lights in the world."

"Anthony Ray Hinton?" One man took a step toward him, yelling his name. Ray noticed that both men each held a hand over the gun at his side. "Police!"

Ray had no idea why there were two policemen on his mama's porch, but he wasn't afraid. He had always been taught: If you haven't done anything wrong, you have no reason to fear and certainly no reason to run. Ray hadn't done anything wrong since he'd gotten out of jail, and he'd kept up his regular parole check-ins. There was nothing to be afraid of.

"We need to talk to you." They flanked Ray on both sides and sort of nudged him down the driveway to their car. It was then that he felt a little twinge at the back of his shoulder blades, and his stomach churned.

"Am I going to jail?"

They patted him down and cuffed his hands behind his back. "I didn't do anything," Ray said loudly. As they started to open up the back door of their car, Ray spoke up again. "What's this about?"

"They will tell you when we get you to Bessemer."

"Can I go in and tell my mom that I'm leaving?" Whatever

this was about, Ray knew it would get cleared up fast. He hadn't done anything wrong.

They walked him up to the side door, and he yelled for his mom.

She opened the door, and Ray and the police officers took a step in.

"They are arresting me. Taking me to jail. Don't worry. I didn't do anything. Don't worry." Ray spoke fast because he could see the confusion on her face, and he didn't want her to start yelling at the police or start crying. Just like that, they turned him around and walked him back to the car. A sergeant named Cole introduced himself and read him his rights.

Then they asked to search his car, and his bedroom. Ray said yes; he had nothing to hide. Maybe this would all be cleared up and he could avoid a trip to jail.

Ray sat with an officer in the car while the other guy searched his car and his room. A few moments later, he walked back out to the car with nothing in his hands. They hadn't found anything. Ray was hoping this meant he could go.

Ray's mom was behind the officer and she started yelling just like she used to do during one of his baseball games.

"That's my baby! That's my baby!"

Only she wasn't cheering, she was crying, almost sobbing, and Ray's hands were behind his back, so he yelled as loud as he could as they swung the car out at the bottom of the driveway.

"It's okay, Mama! It's going to be okay."

As the police car started down the road, away from his mother, Ray felt like his heart was going to crack in two pieces. "It's okay," he mumbled. "It's all going to be okay."

This was all going to work itself out. Ray hadn't done anything wrong. That was the truth, and the truth would set him free so that he could go back home and put his arms around his mama. The police officers weren't speaking and neither would Ray until somebody told him what this was about. Once they told him, he would clear it up, and he would be out of the cuffs and back home.

Home.

Ray just wanted to go home.

Chapter Four

PAYING THE PRICE

"I create an alibi for every single day of my life. I live in fear this could happen to me again."

—Anthony Ray Hinton

The night that a manager at a Quincy's restaurant had been abducted, robbed, and shot, Ray had been quietly working the night shift in a locked warehouse fifteen miles away from the scene of the crime.

Ray didn't know where he was that night in February 1985 when John Davidson was murdered. Had he been fast asleep? Sitting at the kitchen table having a meal with his mom? Joking around with Lester? He didn't know—Ray didn't spend his days developing alibis. He had never even eaten at Mrs. Winner's Chicken & Biscuits in Southside. Since he'd paid his price for the car, he'd kept his promise to stay out of trouble. He worked six days a week, assembling and delivering beds. He didn't do anything too spectacular or exciting, just lived an ordinary life. He couldn't say where he was or what he was doing on that particular night, but he knew for sure he was not out beating and robbing and murdering.

John Davidson's killer had walked away with $2,200. What was the price of a life? Ray wondered just what it was that led the shooter to such a desperate act. Every desperate act has its price. Ray didn't know then that the person who would pay the price was him.

BIRMINGHAM, AUGUST 1985

Newspaper articles detailed the story of Ray's arrest as the "Holdup Suspect Charged with Slayings" of John Davidson and Thomas Wayne Vason. The third man, Sid Smotherman, had been wounded, and said that Ray was the culprit. Ray, who had never even been in a fight, was now "identified" as a cold-blooded killer.

Ray didn't know who called the press or what they had been told, but he had watched enough television to know this was a perp walk and he was the perp. The bright lights, the noise, and the shouting were disorienting and confusing. He was somewhere between annoyed and angry. *How embarrassing*, he thought. For himself and for the police when they had to tell the press they made a mistake.

Inside a room in the police station, they put a blank piece of paper in front of Ray and asked him to sign it.

"Just sign it, and we are going to type up your Miranda rights on it so everyone knows we read you your rights."

Ray knew he hadn't done anything wrong, but he wasn't a fool. There was no way he was going to sign a blank piece of paper. "You know what? I'm an honest person, so if anyone asks me—whether it's a judge or another police officer or anyone—I will tell them that you read me my rights," he said.

The detective put the pen on top of the paper. "We're going to take the cuffs of you, and then you can sign the paper and have a drink, and we'll get this all sorted out right quick."

Ray looked up at the men around him. They looked happy, excited, and like they had a big secret they were just dying to tell. Ray felt the first real twinge of fear. Why did they want him to sign a blank piece of paper?

That wasn't right. None of this was right.

"I'm not going to sign that paper."

Ray said it firmly, and the detectives looked at each other. One of the other detectives picked up the paper. They started firing questions at him.

"Where were you on the night of February 23?"

Ray didn't know.

"What about the night of July 2? Where were you on the night of July 2?"

"I was probably home on the second. I don't remember doing anything else. I was probably home in February too. I don't go out much," he said. "I would have been home with my mom those nights."

"Can you prove it?" the detective said quietly, and Ray felt a shiver go up his spine.

"I can't prove it. Man, could you tell me where you were on some random day in February? Seriously."

"I'm not the one under arrest here."

"Well, I shouldn't be under arrest either. I haven't done nothing wrong. Whatever this is, you guys got the wrong guy." Ray was trying to look cool and calm, but he could feel his heart pounding.

"Where were you on the night of July 25?"

July 25 was just a week earlier. Ray absolutely knew where he was on the twenty-fifth!

"I was at a friend's house a couple of miles from my place. This was on Thursday, right?"

One of the detectives wrote something down in a notebook. "What's the name of your friend?"

Ray gave them her name.

"What time were you at her house?"

"I got there about 8:00 p.m. or so, and I left at 11:15."

"And where were you after 11:15?"

"I drove to my job out in Ensley, and I was at work all night. I worked the night shift. Midnight to 8:00 a.m. Bruno's Warehouse. Although sometimes we got off earlier if we finished the work. I think I got off around 6:00 a.m. that day. That would be the twenty-sixth."

There was nothing but silence after that.

They put Ray behind bars, and that's when he realized he was going to be staying the night. He spent a sleepless night in a cell, then they transported him to the county jail in Birmingham. A Lieutenant Acker rode with him.

"What am I under arrest for, exactly?" Ray asked.

"You want to know why you're under arrest?"

"Yes, I do."

"You're under arrest for first-degree kidnapping, first-degree robbery, first-degree attempted murder."

"Man, you got the wrong person." The man in the headlines, the one the police were talking about, that wasn't him. He was Anthony Ray Hinton. People called him Ray.

"Man, we're not even done with you yet. There's going to be more charges." Acker turned around and looked Ray in the eye. "You know, I don't care whether you did or didn't do it. In fact, I believe you didn't do it. But it doesn't matter. If you didn't do it, one of your brothers did. And you're going to take the rap. You want to know why?"

Ray shook his head.

"I can give you five reasons why they are going to convict you. Do you want to know what they are?"

Ray shook his head again, no, but the lieutenant continued.

"Number one, you're Black. Number two, a white man gonna say you shot him. Number three, you're gonna have a white district attorney. Number four, you're gonna have a white judge. And number five, you're gonna have an all-white jury."

He paused and smiled at Ray. "You know what that spell?"

Ray shook his head, but he'd been raised in the South, he knew. His whole body went numb, like he was under an ice-cold shower in the middle of winter.

"Conviction. Conviction. Conviction. Conviction. Conviction."

Ray closed his eyes.

Ray's mom had taught all of her kids to respect authority. "Tell the truth," she always said, "and you've got nothing to fear." When Ray had gotten in trouble, she said, "Even if it hurts you, you tell the truth. What's done in the dark will always come to light." In his mom's world, the police were who you ran to when you were in trouble—you never ran from them. They were always there to help. That was why Ray had let them search his car and his room. That's why he had told them his mom had a gun when they'd asked. You told the truth. The police were there to help. There was nothing to be afraid of.

Ray thought of her at home alone and scared. He hadn't been offered a phone call. He hoped the neighbors were with her. Ray knew Phoebe, Lester's mom, would be at his mom's side. He wondered if Lester had heard. The only thought that brought Ray some comfort was knowing that Lester would look out for his mom, just like Ray would have done for Lester's mom.

This would get cleared up. First-degree robbery and attempted murder and kidnapping? Ray felt like *he'd* been kidnapped. But it would all get cleared up. They would see he'd been at work. They'd talk to his friend. He couldn't remember the other nights, but he hadn't done anything wrong, so the more he cooperated and helped them investigate whatever this was, the sooner he would go home. He had to believe that. He didn't care what Acker said. No one was going to convict Anthony Ray Hinton of something he didn't do. He was innocent, and it would get sorted out in the morning.

When they got to Birmingham, the press was in front of the Birmingham jail—more lights and flashes as the police paraded Ray around. He was read his rights again and processed into the jail with fingerprints and mug shots and was told they were also charging him with murder. Two murders. They had evidence, they said. The gun at Ray's house matched the bullets. They'd found the murder weapon. It was over. He should confess. None of it made sense. Ray refused to speak. He just wanted a moment to clear his head and sort everything out.

He needed to talk to his mom.

Ray was given green-and-white-striped scrubs to change into, and they took him up to the seventh floor—C block. He was given a one-inch-thick mattress, a plastic razor, a plastic mug, a toothbrush, and his very own roll of toilet paper.

Ray set his stuff down on his bunk. He wanted to lie down and sleep for a week.

That wasn't going to happen.

"Stand outside your cell with your back against the wall."

He lined up with everyone else and watched as the guards did roll call. Ray looked around. There were twenty-three other men there with him. Most were Black; some were white.

When roll call was over, Ray turned to go back into his cell.

"Hinton! You can't go back in your cell until the day's over. Everyone has to be in the common area."

The common area had metal seats and tables bolted to the floor, and all of them were arranged so that they faced a small television mounted to the wall. All Ray wanted to do was call his mom and Lester and see if they could straighten out this mess somehow. And then he wanted to close his eyes and sleep and wake up from this nightmare at home, in his own bed.

Ray sat down on one of the cold, rounded seats and nodded at the white guy who sat down across from him. He had bright red hair, and a big smile that looked half friendly and half serial killer–clown.

"Welcome to C block," he said. "It's where all the capital murder kids come to play."

Chapter Five

ALL Y'ALL

"There's an awful lot about our criminal justice system that is dysfunctional. Everyone who sets foot in a criminal courtroom will see myriad ways the system is dysfunctional."
—**Chesa Boudin, San Francisco District Attorney**

Ray was indicted by a grand jury on November 8, 1985. His face was in all the local newspapers, and the public decided he was guilty. Many were ready to shoot him outright and save the taxpayers some money. And this was all before he had even stepped foot in a courtroom. Before he had been appointed a public defender. And before he was even able to say, "Not guilty," at an arraignment.

Ray's case was assigned to a judge on November 13, 1985—his name was Judge James S. Garrett. When Ray met his court-appointed attorney, Sheldon Perhacs, he heard Perhacs mumble, "I didn't go to law school to do pro bono work."

Ray cleared his throat, and Perhacs looked him in the eye for the first time. Even though he was handcuffed and chained, Ray held out his hand for a shake.

"Would it make a difference if I told you I was innocent?" Ray asked.

"Listen," said Perhacs, "all y'all always doing something and saying you're innocent."

Ray dropped his hand. He was pretty sure that when Perhacs

said "all y'all," he wasn't talking about ex-cons or former coal miners or Geminis or even those accused of capital murder. "All y'all" meant Black people. And Black meant guilty.

Ray knew he wasn't "all y'all," and he wasn't guilty. He was Anthony Ray Hinton. People called him Ray.

Ray let it slide. He had to, he needed Perhacs. He had to believe that Perhacs believed him. He had to believe that Perhacs would fight for him, like Rocky, in the movies. Perhacs was Rocky, and Ray was Apollo Creed—not like in the first movie but in later movies, like *Rocky IV*, even though Ray hadn't seen the movie yet, just the trailer. But it looked like Rocky and Apollo were allies, friends even. Ray wanted to think of Perhacs training early in the morning, running up the courthouse steps, drinking raw eggs while he read through tall stacks of case files, and left no stone unturned in his investigation. It made Ray feel better to pretend that Perhacs truly believed he was in the fight of his life—fighting for Ray's life.

It wasn't until about ten years later that Ray actually got to see *Rocky IV*. Then he was glad that he hadn't known that Apollo Creed died in that movie while Rocky stood by and watched.

The judge set a trial date of March 6, 1986.

"Give me a lie detector test," Ray told Perhacs. "A truth serum. Hypnotize me. Whatever you have to give me that will show them I'm telling the truth. I don't care what it is, I'll take it, I'll do it. This whole thing is a mistake. I'll take any test they have to prove it."

Perhacs just stared at Ray, and then he waved his hand in the air like he was swatting away a fly. "I'll come see you at the jail soon. We'll talk about your case. I promise."

Ray held on to that promise like a drowning man hangs on to whatever he can grab that he thinks will save him. It was all he could do.

Ray took seven different tests.

CONCLUSION:

It is the opinion of this examiner that the subject told the truth during this polygraph examination.

Polygraph examiner, Clyde A. Wolfe

Ray knew he had passed the polygraph. He heard a female guard talking to the examiner while he waited to be brought back to C block.

"How'd he do?"

The examiner answered the guard. "If I could go by this test, he would walk out of here with me right now. He showed no signs of deception. He didn't do it. He doesn't know anything about these murders, I can tell you that for a fact."

Ray heard her grunt in agreement. "You know, I've been doing this for twenty-seven years, and I've seen a lot of killers. He's no killer."

Ray went to sleep that night with new hope. Every day felt like being in the middle of a bad dream. He didn't know how his mom had been able to come up with $350 for the polygraph test, but he knew that as soon as he was out and could get to work, he would earn enough money to pay it back. Ray kept thinking they would catch the person who really did it. It was like the police and the judge and the prosecutors and even his own attorney were in on some bad practical joke, and he was just waiting for them to tell him they had been punking him, that it was some big, horrible, unfunny joke.

When the guard next called him out for a legal visit, he thought Perhacs was finally there to tell him he could go. It was straight out of John 8:32—"And the truth shall set you free." Perhacs had only visited Ray a couple of times in jail, but he had given Ray his phone number and said he could call him whenever he wanted. That was more than most guys in C block got from their court-appointed attorneys. Perhacs and Bob McGregor had made an agreement that whatever happened with the polygraph, whatever the results, either side could use the test to argue their case. If Ray failed, McGregor could use it to convict him, and if he passed, Perhacs could use it to prove his innocence and show them once and for all they had the wrong guy. Ray hadn't worried about making that deal—he knew what the results would be.

Then Perhacs delivered the devastating news. "They're not allowing the polygraph. Bob McGregor nicked on the deal."

Ray watched as Perhacs's mouth kept moving, but it sounded like a swarm of bees had gathered in his head. He couldn't hear anything Perhacs was saying. Betrayal felt like ice under his skin; he went cold and numb. This was real fear. Ray thought back to the days of diving into the ditches with Lester when they walked home. He'd thought that was what fear felt like—his heart pounding and his breath going fast, but this was different. This was ice and steel and a thousand blades carving him up from the inside out. Ray couldn't make sense of what was happening. They knew he didn't do it, but they were still going to take him to trial? They were willing to let the real killer go and pin this on him?

Ray had Perhacs walk him through it all again, slowly.

- All the bullets from the two murders and from the Quincy's robbery matched his mom's gun. Ray knew this was impossible, because that gun hadn't been fired in twenty-five years. A neighbor had been there when the police went back to get the gun from his mom, and she had seen the detective put a cloth inside the gun, and when he pulled it out, he said that it was full of dust and hadn't been fired in a long time.

- The Quincy's victim, Sid Smotherman, had picked Ray out of a photo lineup and said Ray was the guy who robbed him and shot at him. Ray had been at work when this happened. He was signed in. Ray couldn't understand how they were just ignoring this. He had been with other people. His supervisor gave him assignments all night long.

"How could I be in two places at once?" Ray asked Perhacs. "What are they thinking? That's not even possible. There was a guard. I had to check in and out!"

"They are going to say you snuck out. You drove to Quincy's and you robbed him." Perhacs rubbed his hand through his hair.

"That's impossible. When we're at trial, can we ask the judge to have the jury drive the route exactly at midnight and see that the time frame won't work? It's not even possible for me to clock in and get my assignment and get back to Bessemer in a few minutes. It takes at least twenty or twenty-five minutes to get there. Drive the route. Can you get an expert to drive it? Clock it? That'll prove it." Ray's voice was getting louder than he wanted, but this didn't make sense. "We can show them there's a fifteen-foot fence I would have had to have climbed. And show them where the guards are at and how you have to log in and account for your time the whole shift."

"So what, now I have a lawyer for a client?" Perhacs said this slowly, and Ray got the message loud and clear. Let him figure it out. Let him put on the defense. Ray was just supposed to sit back and be a good boy and not make trouble.

What choice did he have?

So Ray laughed it off, but he had to say just one more thing. "I've been reading the papers. You see that there's been other holdups? Other managers getting robbed at closing? I definitely can't be doing that when I'm locked in here."

"Yeah, I'll look into it," replied Perhacs. "They're only paying me $1,000 for this, and hell, I eat $1,000 for breakfast." He laughed, but it wasn't funny.

The other big obstacle was finding a ballistics expert. Ray needed someone to look at the gun and the bullets and get up there and testify. He knew the State was lying about the bullets and his mom's gun, but it wasn't like a judge or a jury was going to believe him. Perhacs had told Ray that the only thing keeping him from a good defense was money, and then he asked Ray if he had anyone who could pay him $15,000 to do the work. Nobody had that kind of money. Ray had been shocked his mom came up with the lie detector money. He told him that much, and then Ray pleaded with him.

"I promise you that once you prove that I didn't do this and I get out, I'll pay you. You have my word on it. If I have to work night and day and holidays and weekends, I will pay you. Please?" Ray knew he was begging, but it didn't matter.

"Anthony, it just don't work like that. What proof do I have you will pay me? You don't have money to hire me, and besides, I was appointed this job by the court. You can't pay me."

Perhacs had been struggling over finding a ballistics expert. The court was only allowing him $500 for each capital case to hire an expert, and he couldn't find anyone to do the work for $1,000. He had until August to find an expert, and it wasn't looking good. It turned out that $15,000 was also the number that would get him a good expert.

Everything depended on those bullets, since they had no other evidence against Ray.

No fingerprints.

No DNA.

No witnesses.

Because Ray had no alibi for the nights of the murders—because he couldn't account for where he was—that made him guilty.

That and the bullets. They weren't even charging Ray for the Quincy's case, only using it to prove he had done the other two because it was of similar plan and design. That was the magic phrase. "Similar plan and design." Ray read the paper every day. There were robberies of similar plan and design happening every week in Birmingham.

Perhacs made it clear that Ray's only shot was an expert who could counter the State's experts. Ray didn't want to do it, but he called his oldest brother, Willie, in Cleveland and asked him for the money.

"Can your attorney for sure get you off if you hire an expert?" he asked.

"I don't think he can say for sure," answered Ray.

"Well, I need to talk to him. I would need some assurance the money would put an end to this. I need him to give me a guarantee so I'm not wasting my money."

His brother hadn't said yes and he hadn't said no, so . . . that was something. Ray tried not to dwell on the fact that if things were reversed . . . Ray would have given the money, no questions asked.

Perhacs couldn't give him that guarantee. Who in their right mind could make any guarantee like that? His brother was raised like Ray—raised to trust the police, the lawyers, and the judges. He was an upright citizen, never had any trouble and never wanted any. Ultimately, he said no. Ray wanted to believe his brother didn't help because he knew Ray didn't do it, and he trusted the courts. Still, it broke Ray's heart. Ray would have moved heaven and earth to help any of his siblings in the same situation. He believed that was just what family did. Did his brother, in some tiny place in the back of his mind, think that Ray was guilty?

It was like everything good was being taken away from him,

one small chunk at a time. Belief. Family. Truth. Faith. Justice. Who would Ray be when this was all over? Would a jury really be fair and impartial? What if he was found guilty? Some days it felt like the whole world, except for Lester and his mom, was conspiring against him.

Ray's life was in Perhacs's hands, so he made sure to call Perhacs later that week just to tell him how much he appreciated him and how great he was doing. He was Ray's only voice, and Ray needed him to show that jury the truth. Show them who Anthony Ray Hinton was—a boy who loved his mama, who grew up in a community that loved him, a man who had never had a violent moment in his life.

Not a man who would hide in the dark to take your money and your life.

Not a cold-blooded killer. Ray was not that man.

He was not that man.

Chapter Six

COURTROOM DRAMA

"We have a system of justice in this country that treats you much better if you're rich and guilty than if you're poor and innocent."
—Bryan Stevenson

JEFFERSON COUNTY COURTHOUSE, SEPTEMBER 12, 1986

When Ray found out how his name had gotten mixed up in this horror, it reminded him that love of money and a thirst for revenge could change someone from the inside out. A jealous acquaintance named Reggie worked at Quincy's, and had said that he knew a guy who fit the description of the man who committed that robbery. Reggie said that man was Ray. For a $5,000 reward, was Reggie willing to lie in a matter of literal life and death?

Reggie didn't look Ray in the eye while he testified under oath. Ray wondered if Reggie really understood that the State wanted to kill him. Or was he, like every other young and poor Black man in Jefferson County, just trying to get a little extra scratch to make it through? Ray couldn't understand how a life could mean so little. They weren't friends, but until that day, Ray had no idea he and Reggie were mortal enemies. Ray watched him on the stand, looking like he felt important, maybe for the first time in his life.

Reggie and Ray had run into each other at the beginning of July, a few weeks before Ray was arrested. They had a harmless conversation, but now Reggie was taking that little bit of truth and creating a whole drama out of it.

Reggie said Ray was outside of Quincy's waiting for him, as if he knew Reggie would be there. He said Ray scared him so much that he reached for his gun he kept in the car. Ray could feel his legs begin to shake as Reggie testified. He was making things up. Straight-up lying under oath.

"All right, anything else?"

Then Reggie testified that Ray had asked him questions about when they closed, and about the manager, as though Ray had been planning his crimes. Complete lies. Ray figured he would have had to be both extremely stupid and a supervillain to have carried out this crime the way they were telling it.

It didn't even make sense, and Ray hoped that his lawyer really understood that. He had told Perhacs about Reggie's jealousy, and he waited for his lawyer to expose everything.

"Mr. White, how're you doing?"

"How're you doing?"

"Mr. White, you know my client. You and he used to play softball together, didn't you?"

"Yes, sir."

"Not on the same team, though?"

"No, sir."

And it went on like that, like a friendly conversation about the weather, and not about lies, and money, and murder. Not about the truth.

Ray went back to his cell every night after trial and replayed the day in his head. They had traced all the bullets—they called

39

it chain of custody—from the victims, to the hospital, to the police, to the crime lab. The police testified about arresting him, conveniently leaving out the blank piece of paper they'd wanted him to sign or the fact that they said the gun hadn't been fired in a long time. Any truths that didn't make Ray out to be a killer were left out or just plain lied about. Ray's only hope was his ballistics expert. Perhacs had hired him with the little amount of money the court provided, and he had done the tests and concluded that the bullets didn't match the gun. Of course, Ray knew they couldn't have, but the State's experts said they had. They were either bad at their job or lying. Even now, it was hard for Ray to truly wrap his mind around the fact that all these people would just lie to put him to death. What had he done to them? Why? The questions kept him up all night. He thought back to when he was arrested, replaying that last afternoon over and over again in his head. Would he have walked to the porch if he had known what was going to happen? Or would he have run?

He'd always believed that innocent men don't run. Except sometimes innocent men need to run. That was true in Alabama and everywhere. If you're poor and Black, sometimes your best and only chance is to run. But where could he have run to? Everything he was and loved and cared about was in a few miles' radius of that house. Would they have shot him? Probably. There was no good end to the running in his mind, but there were nights when it seemed like dying on the pavement would have been a whole lot easier than proving his innocence in a courtroom. He shouldn't have had to prove he was innocent—they were supposed to prove he was guilty—but not in this courtroom.

Ray missed his mom and Lester, and he hated that they had to sit in the courtroom and hear the lies, day after day. Ray had broken up with his girlfriend about a year earlier—he didn't know how long he was going to be caught up in this nightmare, and he didn't want her caught too. He had been in this county jail for what felt like forever, and he couldn't even begin to think about what would come next if he was found guilty. His mind would just shut down when he tried to think on it. Ray had to believe that a miracle would happen. God never fails. His mom had been telling him that since he could walk. God never fails. Ray needed them to catch the guy who had done it. The state had testimony from their firearms experts, Higgins and Yates. Ray needed his ballistics expert to get on that stand and prove that there was no way his mama's old gun could have killed anybody.

The ballistics expert. He was Ray's only hope.

But as it turned out, that expert, Andrew Payne, never had a chance.

He did a great job in his testimony with Perhacs, walking the jury through all the ways that the bullets used in the crimes didn't match Ray's mother's gun. Payne was a bit socially awkward and nerdy, but he did his job. His findings proved that Ray was innocent, and that was what mattered. After Payne testified, Ray felt like a huge weight had been lifted off his chest. He turned and sent a quick smile to his mom and Lester. And then the moment of relief passed. It was the State's turn to cross-examine.

The prosecutor, Mahon, started out easy—nice, almost—but it was a setup right from the get-go.

"It's your testimony, sir, that you have used comparison microscopes in excess of a thousand times?"

"I would say yes, sir, about a thousand times."

"And you were familiar with that comparison microscope that Mr. Yates has?"

"Well, not familiar with it. It's the first time I'd ever used or seen an American Optical."

"American Optical is a pretty obscure brand?"

"Well, I wouldn't say it's an obscure brand but just that I had never operated one before."

And it went downhill from there.

He'd tried to ask the State's experts for help?! *He'd dropped the bullets?!* Ray looked over at Perhacs—Perhacs looked surprised, as though Payne had not told him how badly it went at the lab. How did he not know all this? At one point, Payne seemed to be whining and complaining on the stand that the other experts wouldn't help him. Ray could only watch as a horror show played out before his eyes.

The prosecution began to wind things up. "Mr. Payne, do you have some problem with your vision?"

"Why, yes."

"How many eyes do you have?"

"One."

"That's all."

Ray could do nothing but lay his head down in his arms and cry. At that moment, he knew that the unthinkable was true: He was going to be convicted of murder. He was innocent. And his one-eyed expert had just handed the prosecution a guilty verdict.

Nothing mattered anymore.

This seems dramatic, like a television courtroom drama. Unfortunately, it's real life and what actually happens in courtrooms isn't anything like what is usually shown on TV—even though research shows that we may be heavily influenced by fake TV courts. In its study, "Normalizing Injustice," Color of Change found that "The Crime TV genre, which reaches hundreds of millions of people in America and worldwide, advances debunked ideas about crime, a false hero narrative about law enforcement, and distorted representations about Black people, other people of color and women."

Also from the report:

- This genre influences the public to grant even more authority to police than they already have: to break the rules, to violate our rights, to cage the beast of crime (as they would see it, racial overtones and all).

- Across shows, race was largely invisible as an issue in the workplace and lives of characters, though several series featured central characters played by people of color.

- Almost all series conveyed the impression that change is not needed: They depicted a system that does not actually have serious problems related to race, gender, violence and the abuse of power.

- Because many viewers experience these depictions as realistic representations of the criminal justice system, they undermine the need for reform and legitimize debunked policies, discredited arguments, corrupt decision makers and (what should be) indefensible actions.

- As a result, viewers are led to believe critically overdue reform efforts and policy measures are unnecessary.

- Exposure to consistent inaccurate portrayals may also serve to increase or decrease the empathy viewers have for different types of people and the different realities and experiences they face.[2]

2 https://colorofchange.org/press_release/normalizing-injustice-new
-landmark-study-by-color-of-change-reveals-how-crime-tv-shows-distort
-understanding-of-race-and-the-criminal-justice-system/

Chapter Seven

NIGHTMARE

"Few people familiar with the state of race relations in the United States today would deny that there is a risk of racial prejudice influencing the sentencing decision in the typical capital case: an African-American facing the death penalty for the murder of a prominent white person who is prosecuted by a white prosecutor before a white judge and an all-white or predominantly white jury."

—Stephen B. Bright[3]

JEFFERSON COUNTY JAIL, DECEMBER 10, 1986

Ray's mom always dressed for jail like she was going to church. All decked out in her ivory gloves, green-and-blue-flowered dress, and her wide blue hat rimmed in white lace, she might have seemed ridiculous to some. The prison couldn't have been further from soft organ music and dark, shiny pews. But, like many Black people, Ray's mom knew that a nice outfit and impeccable manners could be defense weapons and a sort of protection. And the more dressed up she was, the more people better watch out: The bigger her hat, the more she meant

---

3 Stephen B. Bright, Symposium, Discrimination, Death and Denial: The Tolerance of Racial Discrimination in Infliction of the Death Penalty, 35 Santa Clara L. Rev. 433 (1995).

business. And sitting across from Ray, dressed to impress and separated from her son by the prison glass, she was armed to the teeth and ready for battle.

Buhlar Hinton never stopped believing in her son. When they spoke, they didn't speak about the fact that he was one court date away from the death chamber. Ray wondered if they were both pretending, or if they were both just so caught up in terror of this nightmare that neither could face what had happened.

"When are you coming home, baby? When are they going to let you come home?"

His mom always asked when "they" were going to let him come home. Ray was the baby of the family—*her* baby. Up until his arrest, they were together every single day. They went to church together. Ate their meals together. Laughed together. Prayed together. Ray's mom had been by his side, cheering him on, for every big moment of his life—baseball games, school exams, dances. She got up early to make him breakfast and pack his lunch when he was going to work in the coal mines, and was there waiting to hug him when he got home, no matter how dusty and dirty he was.

They were everything to each other.

"When are you coming home, baby? When are they going to let you come home?"

At first, from Ray's arrest a year and a half earlier, then during the trial, and even on visiting days, she'd looked kind of dazed and confused by it all. Three months later, she still couldn't understand. How could she? Three months earlier, twelve people had decided that her baby's life was worthless, that the world would be a better place if Ray wasn't in it. That the best thing to do would be to murder him, or, "recommend that he be sentenced to death," which was the nice way of saying something so ugly Ray couldn't even imagine it.

Even though he was living it.

JEFFERSON COUNTY COURTHOUSE, DECEMBER 15, 1986

The Birmingham press had judged Ray guilty from the moment he had been arrested. So had the police detectives, the experts, the prosecutor. And the judge. Ray watched him huff and puff and make a big show out of everything, but yeah, it was just a show. For almost two weeks, the prosecution paraded out witnesses and experts, talked about exhibits A to Z, and pretended that they all hadn't already decided that Ray was guilty. Even his own court-appointed defense attorney believed that Ray, born Black, poor, one of ten children, and robbed of his father for much of his life, was born guilty. Alabama justice wasn't blind. It saw what it wanted to see. Ray didn't have much, but at twenty-nine, he had enough knowledge and experience to understand exactly what kind of justice was being served at his trial. Maybe the good old boys had traded in their white robes for black robes, but the racist, unjust system was the same.

The prosecution was finished. "Your Honor, the State rests."

"All right," said the judge. "Any witnesses for the defense?"

In the prosecution's case, the bailiff had just lied about him under oath, saying that Ray, who had not spoken to anyone but his lawyer about his case for almost two years, had just blurted out a "confession" outside of the courtroom—about cheating on his polygraph test. Supposedly, Ray had gamed the same polygraph test that was not allowed to be used as evidence and, surprise, surprise, proved Ray's innocence. What?! Nothing made sense to Ray anymore.

To Ray's shock, his attorney declined to question the bailiff. Instead, Perhacs turned to him: "Do you want to testify?"

They were about to sentence Ray to death, and nobody was speaking up on his behalf. Did he want to testify?

He was shackled and in leg irons, facing the worst, but there was truth to be told. There were things that needed to go on the record. He wasn't a murderer. Never had been, never would be. Did he want to testify? Ray had spent a good many years testifying for God in church, and now it was time to testify for himself.

His attorney finally showed a little fight and asked if Ray's handcuffs could be removed. It was clear to Ray that he was just another file in a big stack of Perhacs's files. After two years of working on the case, this man didn't know Ray. But Ray had to be polite and respectful, because this man held his life in his hands. His own lawyer probably thought he was guilty, or maybe he didn't care either way. But Ray needed him. They both knew that. Ray had been doing his homework, and if this day went the way he expected it to, he was going to keep needing his lawyer. He was going to keep fighting, and hope that his lawyer would get on board and fight too.

Every day since they had arrested him, he had thought: *Today will be the day. They'll know I was at work. They'll find the guy that really did it. Somebody will believe me.*

It was all some bad dream that he couldn't wake up from.

Ray could feel his heart tighten as he looked at his mom sitting in the courtroom. On her last visit, he'd told her that he'd be home soon to have one of her Sunday afternoon cakes. Sometimes late at night in his cell, Ray would close his eyes and see her red velvet cake with buttercream frosting so clearly in his mind, he swore he could actually smell all that butter and sugar. He'd always had a big imagination. It had helped him get through some rough times growing up, but it had also gotten him into some trouble. Nothing like the trouble he was in now.

Ray smiled at his mom even though he was scared to death. He didn't want to die. But on the outside, he had to be strong. For his mom. For his friends. Martin Luther King, Jr., once said, "A man can't ride you unless your back is bent." So when Judge McGregor tried to stare him down, Ray sat straight up and stared right back. Ray wasn't going to make it easy for them to murder him.

Ray took a deep breath, closed his eyes, and said the same prayer he had prayed in his head a thousand times.

Dear God, let them know the truth of things. Let them see into my mind and my heart and find the truth. Bless the judge. Bless the DA. Bless the victims' families who are in pain. Dear God, let there be justice. Real justice.

Then he began to testify: "First of all, I did not kill anybody. It is important to me that the families know this. Believe this. I wouldn't want anyone to take the life of someone I loved. I couldn't even imagine that pain. I know what it is like not to have a father, to be brought up with that missing in your life, and I wouldn't cause it to happen for anyone. There is a man up above who knows I didn't do it, and one day, I may not be here, but he's going to show you that I didn't do it. I wouldn't dare ever think about killing, because I can't give a life and, therefore, I don't have a right to take a life."

Ray's voice shook.

"And if you . . . if the family's satisfied that they've got the right man, I'm sorry, but if you really want your husband's killer to be brought to justice, get on your knees and pray to God about it, because I didn't do it."

Ray looked right at Judge Garrett.

"Do with me what seems good to you, but as sure as you put me to death, you bring blood upon yourself and upon your hands. I love all people. I've never been prejudiced in this life. I went to school and got along with everybody, never been in a fight. I'm not a violent person.

"You all sent an innocent man to prison. You kept an innocent man locked up for two years, and I begged, I pleaded with you to give me anything that you believe in. Truth serum, hypnosis, anything. I have nothing to hide."

Now Ray looked right at the prosecutor: McGregor.

"I'm praying that God will forgive you all for what you have done, and I hope that you have enough wisdom to ask God to forgive you. You're going to die just like I'm going to die. My death may be in the electric chair, but you're going to die too. But one thing—after my death, I'm going to heaven. Where are you going?"

He looked at the judge and the bailiffs and the district attorney and the police detectives and he asked again.

"Where are *you* going?"

He spoke to the family of the murdered man.

"If I had killed somebody, you wouldn't have found me in

my mama's backyard cutting grass. I had nothing to hide, and I didn't know anything about these murders."

Ray was going to get it all out. He didn't know when he'd have another opportunity like this again.

"Since I been in jail, I've read the paper every day, and hardly a day goes by where people haven't been forced in a cooler, and you going to read about it again. Somebody's going to get killed. Maybe by then, you're going to realize you got the wrong man. But I pray to God it don't happen that way. I just pray that the man that really did it—I just hope the Lord will put enough burden on their heart where they can just come and tell you. But then, I'm not convinced you going to want to believe them. But when God is in the plan, I ain't worried about what you believe. I don't want to be electrocuted, but whatever way the Lord have me go, I'm ready to go. And you know I looked and I've seen prejudice in this courtroom. You people don't want the truth. You people don't want the right person. All you wanted was a conviction."

He looked directly into McGregor's eyes.

"I'm just one Black man, and that don't mean nothing to you. I don't know what color God is, but I can tell you he loves me just like he loves you. You might think you're superior in this world, but you're not. I had a life just like everybody else had a life, and I don't hate you. Mr. McGregor, I don't hate you. But for a slight moment during the trial, I was beginning to hate you, I really was, but I thank God that it came to me that I can't make it into heaven hating nobody."

Ray knew who he was and how he was raised. He knew right from wrong. And this, this was all wrong.

Ray looked at all of those people who seemed as though

they'd enjoyed doing all this wrong . . . and he told them he loved them. They had prosecuted him and were working to kill him, but Ray said:

"I love you."

They were trying to take his life, but they could not steal his heart.

"Might sound crazy, but I got joy—even with leg irons on me. The joy I got—the world didn't give it to me, and the world can't take it away. That's a fact. Your Honor, I thank you for letting me have my say. Mr. McGregor, I'm praying for you real hard."

He went on: "Wherever they send me, God can hear my prayers. Now, what would really make me worried is if you could isolate me from God, but you can't do that. You took me from my family, but you can't take me from God."

Ray knew that, as a Black man, the deck had been stacked against him from the start. Justice wasn't for people like him. "It's sad when a police officer that is supposed to uphold the law tells you you're going to be convicted because you're Black, and you got a white jury and you got a white DA. You know, that's sad. It's sad—real sad. If you talk to Lieutenant Doug Acker, tell him I'm praying for him also."

Ray paused and took one more deep breath. Someday they would know he didn't do it. And then what? What would they all say then? Ray knew what he was going to do now. He sat up as straight as he could. He wasn't going to beg for his life.

"I'm not worried about that death chair," he said. "You can sentence me to it, but you can't take my life. It don't belong to you. My soul, you can't touch it."

After a brief recess, just three hours, it was time.

The judge banged his gavel. Cleared his throat. "It is the

judgment of the court that the defendant, Anthony Ray Hinton, in each of these cases is guilty of the capital offense in accordance with the verdict of the jury in each of these cases. And it is the judgment of the court and the sentence of the court that the defendant, Anthony Ray Hinton, suffer death by electrocution on a date to be set by the Alabama Supreme Court pursuant to Alabama Rules of Appellate Procedure 8-D (1)."

Electrocution.

"The sheriff of Jefferson County, Alabama, is directed to deliver the defendant, the said Anthony Ray Hinton, into the custody of the director of the Department of Corrections and Institutions at Montgomery, Alabama, and the designated electrocution shall, at the proper place for the electrocution of one sentenced to suffer death by electrocution, cause a current of electricity of sufficient intensity to cause death and the application and continuance of such current to pass through the body of said Anthony Ray Hinton until the said Anthony Ray Hinton is dead."

Until he was dead.

Ray heard his mother cry out; he tried to go to her, but the bailiffs held him tight. There was no way for him to comfort his mama. They would kill him right there if they could, and Ray couldn't let them. He needed to survive to get back to his mother. He was her baby, and he was innocent.

They had just decided to kill him. It was all too much for Ray to bear so he prayed to himself.

Dear God, please let the truth be known.
Dear God, do not let me die this way.
Dear God, I am innocent.

Dear God, protect my mom. I am innocent.
I am innocent.

It took the jury two hours to find Ray guilty.

It took them forty-five minutes to determine his punishment.

Death. State-sanctioned killing.

Anthony Ray Hinton was sentenced to die.

In that moment, Ray felt his whole life shatter into a million jagged pieces. The world was fractured and broken, and everything good in him broke with it.

He was Anthony Ray Hinton. People called him Ray.

HALLS OF INJUSTICE

"Race still influences who is sentenced to death and executed in America today . . . In capital trials, the accused is often the only person of color in the courtroom. Illegal racial discrimination in jury selection is widespread, especially in the South and in capital cases—thousands of Black people called for jury service have been illegally excluded from juries."[4]

- In his one-term presidency, Donald Trump appointed over 200 federal judges, "including nearly as many powerful federal appeals court judges in four years as Barack Obama appointed in eight."[5] Current U.S. Associate

---

4 EJI https://eji.org/issues/death-penalty/#Racial_Bias

5 www.pewresearch.org/fact-tank/2021/01/13/how-trump-compares-with-other-recent-presidents-in-appointing-federal-judges/

Attorney General Vanita Gupta pointed out that Trump's picks, made in collaboration with Senate Republicans, were primarily young white men. "By her count, nearly 7 in 10 of the Trump judges are white men. Just 28 of the 200 are people of color. And, she said, there's only one Latina appeals court judge, and no Black appellate judges."[6] Federal judges can stay on the job for the rest of their lives.

- Jurors in Washington State are three times more likely to recommend a death sentence for a Black defendant than for a white defendant in a similar case. (Prof. K. Beckett, Univ. of Washington, 2014)

- In Louisiana, the odds of a death sentence were 97 percent higher for those whose victim was white than for those whose victim was Black. (Pierce & Radelet, *Louisiana Law Review*, 2011)[7]

- In 2014, a study found that 95 percent of elected state and local prosecutors in the country were white. 79 percent were white men, even though white men make up 31 percent of the U.S. population.[8]

- "Across all Article III U.S. District Courts and the U.S. Courts of Appeals, people of color make up just 20

6 www.npr.org/2020/07/02/886285772/trump-and-mcconnell-via-swath-of-judges-will-affect-u-s-law-for-decades

7 https://deathpenaltyinfo.org/

8 www.nytimes.com/2015/07/07/us/a-study-documents-the-paucity-of-black-elected-prosecutors-zero-in-most-states.html?_r=0

percent of all sitting judges and 27 percent of active judges. In all, African Americans comprise 10 percent of sitting judges and 13 percent of active judges, while Hispanic judges make up about 7 percent and 9 percent of sitting and active judges, respectively. Asian Americans comprise an even smaller proportion of the lower federal courts: Only 2.5 percent of active judges and 4 percent of sitting judges are Asian American. American Indian judges and those belonging to more than one race or ethnicity each make up about 1 percent or less of the lower federal judiciary."[9]

• "Among active judges, women make up at least half of the bench on 15 district courts—16 percent [of the district courts in the country]—and the majority of the bench on just 7 district courts, or 8 percent. Just one district court—the Southern District Court of Illinois—entirely comprises active female judges. Active judges who self-identify as LGBTQ are completely absent from 90 percent of all federal district courts."[10]

• "Sixty percent, or 55 out of 91, of all Article III district courts have no women of color actively serving on them. There are only two district courts—the Southern District Court of Illinois and the District Court of Hawaii—where women of color make up half of presiding active judges."[11]

9 www.americanprogress.org/issues/courts/reports/2020/02/13/480112 /examining-demographic-compositions-u-s-circuit-district-courts/

10 Ibid.

11 Ibid.

The state of Alabama wanted to murder Ray because they'd decided he had murdered two people and tried to murder a third.

Only they had the wrong guy.

Ray knew they had the wrong guy. His mother knew they had the wrong guy. Lester, who had been his best friend since Ray was six and Lester was four—Lester knew they had the wrong guy.

Some of them even said they knew they had the wrong guy.

But it didn't seem to matter. Ray had been born Black and poor in the state of Alabama, and it seemed like his very existence was a crime.

The trial had been like drowning in an overwhelming sea of wood and white faces. Sitting in that courtroom day after day, Ray felt like an uninvited guest in a rich man's library. Even though he knew he was innocent, he felt shame, like he was coated in something dirty and evil. It felt like the whole world thought he was bad, and that made it hard to hang on to his goodness. He was trying, though. The Lord knew how hard he was trying.

He had gone on trial for a crime that he couldn't even fathom, his heart breaking because his mom was there in the courtroom in her best dress and big heart, smiling because she believed in her son. Always had, always would. Even though a jury had found Ray guilty of murder, she still believed in him. She and Lester didn't care that the press made Ray out to be some kind of monster. They knew the truth: Ray was innocent.

Every week, Lester was the first in line on visiting day, stopping in on his way to work to say hello to Ray and leave some money in his account so Ray had the essentials—toilet paper, toothpaste. Every single week, for a year and a half. No matter what. He really was the best, best friend a guy could have.

Ray vowed that he would come home someday, and he knew Lester would help his mom hold on to that homecoming hope. He didn't want his mom to lose her hope. There was no sadder place to be in the world than a place where there's no hope. After a year and a half in that jail, and now that he had been "sentenced to death," Ray knew that.

It was almost too much for Ray, an innocent man sentenced to death, just thinking about the fact that those two people never doubted him for a second, that they loved him so hard and so long—it made a lump form in his throat. Ray knew that even if he were guilty, even if he had murdered those two people in cold blood for a little cash, his mom and Lester would have still loved and believed in him.

They loved him that much.

"When are you coming home, baby?"

"Soon, Mama," Ray always said. "They're working on it. I plan to be home soon."

Ray prayed, and he would pray again. Pray for the truth. Pray for the victims. He prayed for his mom and for Lester. And he prayed that the nightmare he had been living for almost two years would end somehow. He would still pray for a miracle and try not to criticize it if the miracle didn't look like what he expected.

That's what his mama had always taught him.

Now, Ray knew that the best chance for his life was to be sentenced to death. Every poor person tangled up in the legal system knew this. By sentencing him to death, they were giving Ray the only shot he had at proving his innocence. Now that he was sentenced to die, he would be guaranteed an appeal and guaranteed some representation by his attorney. The law said that if he had been sentenced to life in prison, he would have had to hire an attorney to appeal. Ray had no money to prove his innocence.

So he was headed to Holman Prison. *The House of Pain. Dead Man Land. The Slaughter Pen of the South.* It had a lot of names. He was terrified, but ready to fight. He knew the only way to fight this injustice would be from inside.

God have mercy on my soul.

Chapter Eight

THE PRICE OF INNOCENCE

"They have cheated him out of his ballot, deprived him of civil rights or redress therefor in the civil courts, robbed him of the fruits of his labor, and are still murdering, burning and lynching him. The result is a growing disregard of human life . . . The South is brutalized to a degree not realized by its own inhabitants, and the very foundation of government, law and order, are imperilled."
—**Ida B. Wells,** *Southern Horrors: Lynch Law in All Its Phases*

BIRMINGHAM, DECEMBER 17, 1986

The twenty-four-hour gap between when the judge sentenced Ray to death and when they came to take him to Holman Prison where he'd wait to be killed was a blur. He was in shock. He was officially a condemned man, and none of the guards or the other inmates would meet his eye. It was like the death penalty was a contagious disease and everyone thought they could catch it from him. Anthony Ray Hinton was now officially the worst of the worst. A human not fit for this life. Ray could feel a rage inside him bubbling below the surface. He was a child of God who was condemned to die. He couldn't wrap his brain around it. How did he get here?

His cell in the county jail had been home for the past year and a half. Some guys who came in after Ray had already been tried and gone up to death row in Holman, and others were given life sentences. Hardly anyone was found innocent. The guys in C block who had money seemed to come in and go out a lot faster than the guys like Ray who were poor. If you had a court-appointed lawyer, like Perhacs, your case always seemed to be delayed, trial dates moved back, hearings postponed.

Why do we judge some people less worthy of justice?

Why does innocence have a price?

Decades of racial terror in the American South reflected and reinforced a view that African Americans were dangerous criminals who posed a threat to innocent white citizens . . . By 1915, court-ordered executions outpaced lynchings in the former slave states for the first time. Two-thirds of those executed in the 1930s were Black, and the trend continued. As African Americans fell to just 22 percent of the South's population between 1910 and 1950, they constituted 75 percent of those executed in the South during that period . . . Race remains a significant factor in capital sentencing. African Americans make up less than 13 percent of the nation's population, but nearly 42 percent of those currently on death row in America are Black, and 34 percent of those executed since 1976 have been Black. In 96 percent of states where researchers have completed studies examining the relationship between race and the death penalty, results reveal a pattern of discrimination based on the race of the victim, the race of the defendant, or both.

—Lynching in America, EJI

In 1916, the NAACP partnered with a group called the Anti-Lynching Crusaders to wage a campaign against the brutal practice of lynching and advocate for antilynching legislation. The **Dyer Bill**, named for Missouri Republican Representative Leonidas Dyer, an opponent of lynching, passed the House in 1918 but was stalled in the Senate by Southern Democrats. In 1934, Senate Democrats Robert F. Wagner (NY) and Edward Costigan (CO) tried again with the **Costigan-Wagner Bill**, which aimed for federal prosecution of lynch mobs. Concerned that it would turn off white Southern voters, President Franklin D. Roosevelt balked at publicly supporting the bill, and it went nowhere. Public pressure—and lynchings—continued. It was not until 2018 that the Senate passed the **Justice for Victims of Lynching Act**, introduced by Senators Kamala Harris, Cory Booker, and Tim Scott; it was not passed by the House.[12] In 2005, the Senate passed a resolution apologizing for the absence of antilynching legislation. In 2020, the House revised the **Justice for Victims of Lynching Act** and passed the **Emmett Till Antilynching Act**, which, as of May 2021, has been stalled in the Senate, primarily due to the opposition of Republican Senator Rand Paul of Kentucky. As of 2021, Congress has not passed any federal antilynching legislation in the United States.[13]

---

12 www.bbc.com/news/world-us-canada-44668459

13 www.washingtonpost.com/powerpost/sen-paul-acknowledges-holding-up-anti-lynching-bill-says-he-fears-it-would-be-wrongly-applied/2020/06/03/29b97330-a5bf-11ea-b619-3f9133bbb482_story.html

The van for death row came on Mondays and Thursdays, so Ray figured it would be the following Monday before he left. He hadn't been able to use the phone since his sentencing, and he wanted to talk to his mom and Lester. He wanted to make sure his mom was okay. He wanted to tell her *he* was okay so she wouldn't worry.

He wasn't okay, though. How could he be? For the thirty-six hours since he'd left that courtroom, Ray had been replaying every word of the trial and sentencing in his head. He hadn't slept, he hadn't eaten, and he hadn't talked to anybody. Perhacs had told the judge and prosecutors that he had gotten a call at his office and at his home from a guy saying he was the real killer, and nobody had tracked that down. They'd had a discussion about it with the jury out of the room, but nobody cared. Nobody had hunted that man down. Were they all in on it? How did they get people to lie for them? The bailiffs had lied. Reggie had lied. Clark Hayes, a grocery clerk Ray didn't even know, had lied when he said he saw Ray following Smotherman around Food World. The State's firearms experts, Higgins and Yates, had lied or they just plain got it wrong—there was no way those bullets matched his mom's gun. Ray thought about poor Payne, the "ballistics expert" who was destroyed on that stand, humiliated, mocked, and made to look like a liar himself.

Around and around and around, the scenes from the trial swirled in his head. His lawyer had just let the jury sentence him to death without any discussion or testimony. Why hadn't Perhacs put up his mom and Lester, his neighbor, his church family to tell the jury who Ray was and what he was about? Ray didn't understand at all. He hoped Perhacs did better with his appeal—Ray was innocent, and his lawyer knew it. The lie detector test proved it!

Ray couldn't even wrap his brain around what death row was going to be like. He'd been in prison for over a year, and he wanted to go home. He wanted to cut his mom's grass and sit with her outside at sunset. He wanted to take her fishing. Why hadn't he gone fishing with her more when she loved it so much? How was she going to get around? Who was going to help her keep up the house? Ray knew Lester would help, but that wasn't the same. Ray—her son, her baby—he wanted to do it; it was his job.

He missed his girlfriend, Sylvia. He missed her sweet kisses and her skin that smelled like spring flowers after the rain. Ray hadn't smelled anything good in a year and a half. The sweat of men forced to wear the same clothes for weeks at a time was all that filled his nostrils. He wanted to feel the rain on his neck, the sun on his face. He wanted to take a simple walk at sunrise. He wanted to play baseball and basketball. He wanted to drink sweet tea and eat his mom's grits and, Lord, he wanted some of her cobbler. He hadn't had real food in so long. He wanted his simple life back. He wanted to be treated like a human being. After living in his cage of a cell, Ray wanted to travel to all the places he used to imagine visiting, the places he'd thought that he might get to see one day. Places like Hawaii, England, and South America. He wanted to get married and have children and show them the same kind of love he had had as a kid. He didn't want to be watched when he was in bed, in the bathroom, every second. He wanted to laugh. He wanted to be free.

He wanted to kill the prosecutor, McGregor.

The knowledge that he was capable of those thoughts hit

Ray like a sucker punch to his gut. It scared him. This was not him, this wanting to kill. What had they done to him?

He wanted to murder McGregor the way McGregor had murdered Ray's life. Ray wanted to make it so McGregor could never hurt another person again, until every last lie in him died with him.

He hadn't come into this jail a murderer; was he going to let them turn him into one?

"Hinton, all the way! Hinton, all the way!"

It was time. Ray heard the automatic lock click on his cell door as it opened. "All the way" meant to pack everything up. He couldn't believe they were taking him so soon. He wasn't ready to go to Holman Prison. He hadn't talked to his mom.

"Hinton, all the way! Get a move on!"

Ray packed up some legal papers and a few pictures. He didn't know what else he could take, so he left his commissary behind for whoever wanted it. He knew that when the other guys woke up, they would be all over his cell like vultures to take whatever he had left behind.

"Let's go, Hinton."

Ray was supposed to roll up his mattress and bring his sheet and blanket, but he just left them there. He wasn't going to follow the rules anymore. He had done that, and look where it had gotten him. They said he was the worst of the worst? Maybe it was time he started acting like it.

They put Ray in a holding cell and gave him a breakfast of congealed eggs and a hard biscuit and jelly. He was strip-searched and chained, extra-heavy chains around his waist that were attached to the metal cuffs on his wrists and ankles. Ray could barely walk. He wondered who had sat around and said to himself, "I should invent something that will chain a man like an animal and make those chains so heavy he can't hold up his arms or move his legs." Ray hated that person too.

The guards who walked Ray out to the van tried to chitchat with him, but Ray said nothing. They looked uneasy. Ray had been nice and cooperative since he'd been there. But no more. He wasn't going to make their jobs any easier. He let himself go limp when they tried to hoist him up the first step of the van. Ray weighed over two hundred pounds. Let them lift him. He would let them feel his weight as they carted him off to his death. He was somebody. He was a person. He was going to make them feel it.

After he finally got into the van, Ray didn't say a word. He wasn't going to speak to them or to anyone ever again. What was the point? When no one believes a word you say, the best thing to do is stop talking.

The ride to Holman took over three hours. Ray had never been that far south before, and it felt like a ride to the end of the world. Two guards sat up front, and there was a mesh cage separating Ray from them. The windows had wire mesh over them as well, but Ray could see out. He hadn't been given a chance to call anyone before they'd left; no opportunity for goodbyes to his mom and Lester. Ray hated them even more for not giving him that chance. The guards were joking and laughing up front, and he watched the countryside he loved pass by. Would he ever feel grass under his feet again?

Ray had always said this was God's country, but where was God now? Ray was chained and shackled like an enslaved man being taken to auction.

He was cargo, less than human.

When something good happened to a neighbor, his mom always said, "God blessed this family. God did this for our neighbor. Praise be to God for looking out for that family." If God blessed people, then did he also punish people? Ray wanted to know why God was punishing him. Why had God blessed that person but put him in the back of a van, wrapped in chains?

What had Ray ever done to God?

Ray imagined the van crashing and rolling over and over again so that his chains came off and he could escape. He would run and run and run until there was no death penalty and he wasn't a condemned man. He would keep running until he was out of Alabama and in some place where freedom was real and his life couldn't be taken away from him.

It had been a long time since Ray had seen cars and people and open road and open sky. As they went on, he tried to capture pictures in his mind. A little boy looking bored in the back seat of a station wagon. A pretty girl driving a blue car. A restaurant with a CLOSED sign. A family laughing as they whizzed past. There was a whole world out there enjoying a Wednesday morning, without fear. They were free to do what they wanted, and Ray wondered if they understood what that meant. He saw a Black man, about his age, drive by in a Buick.

"Watch out," Ray murmured out loud. "They're going to come for you too. Hey!" he yelled up to the guards.

"What?"

"I have to go to the bathroom."

Eventually, they pulled into a store with a gas station out front. They parked around the side, and one guard took Ray into the bathroom while the other went and filled up with gas.

Ray could see some Black kids outside the store staring at him like he was a strange animal in the zoo. Ray wanted them to see what a Black man looked like chained from head to toe. He wanted them to remember.

When they pulled up to the parking lot of Holman Prison, Ray saw inmates on the other side of a tall wire fence. Two guards opened a big gate, and they drove through. Guards brought Ray in through a heavy door and took the chains off but cuffed his hands. He was at the place where they wanted him to die.

"He's all yours," the county guard said, and turned Ray over to a short, squat man with long sideburns and a comb-over.

They sat him down in a chair and asked for his name.

Ray said nothing.

"What's your social?"

Ray just shrugged.

The guard read it off a paper. "Is that your social?"

Ray nodded. He wasn't going to talk to them. He wasn't going to make this easy.

"We're gonna send you to the infirmary to get checked out, and then you'll get a real physical at another time. You gonna put these whites on, and then you'll be escorted to your cell."

Ray didn't say a word.

He changed into a white prison jumpsuit that said ALABAMA DEPARTMENT OF CORRECTIONS on the back. He was given his inmate number—Z468.

He was Anthony Ray Hinton. People called him Ray.

The infirmary weighed him, asked if he took any medication, if he was on drugs. If he had any medical problems they needed to know about.

Ray shook his head to everything they asked but still didn't speak.

After his medical examination, he was brought down a hall. There were some other inmates in the hall, but they were told to turn and face the wall with their noses against it. Ray couldn't understand why they did this, but then he saw one of the guys look up at him from the wall, and Ray saw fear in his eyes.

The guard started yelling at the other inmate, who was a white man, about Ray's age. "Don't look at him! You can't look at him! On your knees! On your knees, hands behind your back, nose against the wall! All of you!"

Ray had no idea what was going on or why the guard reacted that way. Then it hit him. They all thought he might attack. The regular inmates were being protected from the death row inmate. Ray was the scariest person in that prison.

Ray was taken to another guard—the captain of the guards. He told Ray he was in charge of death row.

"I didn't ask for you to come here, and I have but one job, and that's to keep you here. As long as you are at Holman Prison, you are going to see these blue uniforms and you are going to respect them. You will abide by the rules and regulations and do anything these blue uniforms tell you to do. Is that clear?"

Ray nodded.

"Now, you can make it easy on yourself or you can make it hard on yourself. However you decide to do it. You are on ninety-day probation. You will be cuffed at all times when you are out of your cell. If we get no trouble, you can have the cuffs off when you shower and when you walk. You walk fifteen minutes a day in a cage on the yard. The rest of the time, you are in your cell. We don't want no trouble. Okay?"

Fifteen minutes. In a cage on the yard.

Ray kept his eyes down and nodded again.

"Sergeant, take him to his cell."

They walked Ray down a long hall and through a doorway that said DEATH ROW at the top. They walked up a flight of stairs, and the guard started yelling out row numbers. Finally, he stopped in front of cell number 8.

"Number 8!" he yelled.

Ray heard a voice from behind them call the number back, and then there was a loud clank and the door opened. Inside was a small, narrow bunk with a thin plastic mattress. Another guard walked in and put a sheet, blanket, towel, and washcloth on the bed. He also set down a brown bag of Ray's stuff from the county jail. It had his Bible, some letters, and legal papers from his trial. He could hear guys yelling, and he saw some mirrors sticking out of the other cells—that was so the inmates could see what was going on, who the guards were bringing in.

From somewhere far off, Ray could hear a man screaming. Another man was laughing. Another one just kept saying, "Hey! Hey! Hey!" over and over again.

Ray walked into the cell, and the guards stepped out.

"When we close the door, stick your hands out through here and we'll take off the cuffs."

Ray didn't say anything and the guard gave him a look, then continued. "It's too late for you to order a Christmas package this year, but maybe next year."

Christmas? The last thing Ray was thinking about was Christmas. He didn't want to order a Christmas package, and he didn't want to celebrate Jesus's birthday. What was the point?

The door slammed shut, and the sounds began to echo in

Ray's head. He could feel his stomach doing flips, and his knees began to shake. He thought he might throw up. He stuck his hands through the small slot so the guards could take off the cuffs. He flexed his wrists and turned back around to face his new home: his cell. It was five feet wide and about seven feet long. A metal toilet with a sink on top, and a shelf and the bed.

That was it.

Ray sat down on the edge of the bed and looked in the bag of his stuff. He pulled out the King James Bible. All of it was a lie. There was no God for him anymore. His God had forsaken him. His God didn't love him. His God was a punishing God who had failed and left him to die. Ray had no use for God. *Forgive me, Mama*, he thought to himself as he threw the Bible under the bed.

Ray didn't bother making his bed; he just lay down and closed his eyes. When they tried to pass his dinner through the slot in his door, Ray didn't bother getting up to take it. He wasn't going to talk to anyone or take anything from anyone. He was full of a hate too big for that little cell.

He was completely alone.

Ray decided he would find a way to escape, and find a way to put right all that had been made wrong. He would prove his innocence.

He would get his revenge. He lay there for hours until he woke up in darkness, except for a light coming from outside his cell.

The only other sound was someone on death row screaming out in the darkness.

"No, no, no, no, noooo!"

Ray pressed his hands against his ears, but the screaming went on.

It never stopped.

71

Chapter Nine

DYING INSIDE

"I've never thought what I do, I do just for my clients or I'm doing just for the people who I represent or the people who know I care about them. I've always felt like my work, our work, is for everybody. That is, we're trying to save everyone from the corruption, from the agony of living lives where there is no mercy, where there is no grace, where there is no justice, where we are indifferent to suffering. Those kinds of lives ultimately lead to violence and animosity and bigotry, and I don't want that for anybody."

—Bryan Stevenson[14]

There is no "Welcome to Your Appeal" brochure that prisoners get after they are condemned. Nobody sits them down and explains what has to be filed and how much time they have to file it. A prisoner is guaranteed a direct appeal to the State appellate courts—the Court of Criminal Appeals and the Alabama Supreme Court—but that's really it. The State of Alabama does not want to make it easy, and they offer zero assistance to death row inmates. Unfairly convicted? Prejudiced at trial? Confession coerced? Constitutional rights violated? Your attorney sucked? Good luck with that. There is no post-conviction help

---

14 https://onbeing.org/programs/bryan-stevenson-finding-the-courage-for-whats-redemptive/

for the condemned. They are on their own, like Ray, and the State does everything it can to make it difficult with a whole lot of obscure procedures and rules that seem to prevent prisoners from revisiting anything once a court has ruled on it.

And in Alabama, judges are elected based on how many people they send to death row, not on how many people they let off.

Ray called Perhacs's office whenever he could, and his secretary assured him that Perhacs was working on Ray's appeal and promised to give him the messages. Ray had read about robberies in Birmingham that fit the same description as Quincy's, Mrs. Winner's, and another at a place called Captain D's. The Cooler Killer hadn't slowed down at all, and the times when there was a suspect description, it was the same as Smotherman's—Black male, five foot eleven, 180 pounds. Nothing like Ray.

Somehow, it hadn't mattered that he was six foot two and 230 pounds, and it didn't matter that he was locked up and still, the same crimes kept happening. Ray wondered if the victims' families were reading the papers too. Did they ever wonder if the State had convicted the wrong man? Ray sent Perhacs a note along with every crime report he found in the paper. "Just trying to help," he wrote. "Thank you so much!"

Ray wondered if the case ever kept Perhacs awake at night. What was it like for him knowing his client was innocent and sleeping on death row? Ray didn't know at the time that his mom had started writing Perhacs letters too, pleading and begging for him to save her baby's life. Asking him to protect her boy. She wasn't at all happy with what was said about her Ray in court.

Their neighbor Miss Wesley Mae brought Ray's mom to see him at Holman after his ninety-day probation was over and he was allowed a visit. The two old ladies had never before driven so far alone, and had gotten lost trying to find their way to the prison. They showed up on a Friday night, two hours after visiting time was over—but the warden had a little bit of sympathy for them in their Sunday best making their way to the prison, so he let Ray have a visit for about twenty minutes.

Ray hugged his mom as long as he could—another thing that wasn't usually allowed. She smelled like laundry soap and rose water, but she looked tired. There were dark circles under her eyes, and Ray could see new lines around her mouth that weren't there a few months ago.

"God will fix this," she kept saying. "God can do everything but fail, baby. God is going to fix this right up for you."

"Yes, Mama," Ray said. The guard looked up, surprised to hear Ray speak for the first time. Ray didn't have the heart to tell his mom that he was done with God. God didn't live in this place. If there was a God and he thought it was okay to send Ray to hell while he was still alive, well then, he wasn't Ray's God. Not anymore. Not ever again. "You come with Lester next time. I don't want you two driving all this way alone. You got that?"

"You okay, baby?" His mom reached her hand out and touched his cheek. Her eyes filled with tears.

"I'm okay, Mama. Don't you be worrying about me. This place is fine. They are treating me real fine." Ray knew it was wrong to lie to her, but lies told to ease pain or protect someone's heart are lies that need to be told. She already had to live apart from him. If Alabama had its way, she was going to have to live through the unimaginable: them putting Ray to death. He was going to comfort her every single moment that he could, even if it meant telling a million lies. "Now, we only have a few minutes. Don't spend them crying. I'm just fine, but I could use some of your cooking. I could use a nice, juicy hamburger right now."

His mama laughed, and he tried to memorize that sound in his mind. He wanted to hang on to that laugh and hear it in his head instead of the endless moaning he heard all day, every day on the row.

"Your attorney sent me a couple of letters. He's going to get you out of here. He's working real hard."

She carefully unfolded two letters she had brought in. They were addressed to her. Ray hadn't heard from Perhacs yet, but when he'd called his office, his secretary said that he had filed a motion for a new trial.

Ray looked at the first letter. It was dated a few weeks before his sentencing.

"Mama, this first letter is from before I came here."

"Well, I been writing him so he knows who you are. I wanted to tell him that what they said at your trial was a lie. They lied on your name. My son is no killer." She dabbed at her eyes with a white handkerchief.

"It's okay. It's okay." He patted her hand. "Let me have a look."

November 25, 1986

Dear Ms. Hinton:

Thank you for your letter dated November 17, 1986. I want you to know that I will continue to do everything I know how to do to protect your son. His case is going to be appealed,

and I think I'm going to win the appeal. The appeal will
probably take a couple of years. After that, we will probably
have to try his case again. The next time we try it, we will do
some things differently. I still think he has a good opportunity
to be acquitted of these charges.

I will continue to do everything I know how to do.

Sincerely, Sheldon Perhacs

Ray didn't want to sit on death row for a couple of years. Perhacs would do some things differently next time? How about getting a competent ballistics expert? Ray still cringed when he thought about his expert getting crucified on the stand. Would they give them more money for a better expert if they tried him again? It seemed like if you were poor, you were as good as guilty. Ray picked up the second letter. It was dated just a month earlier.

March 2, 1987

Dear Ms. Hinton:

I intend to continue to do everything I know how to do to
protect your son. The case is in the process of being appealed.
The appeal will take quite some time to complete. It is my
opinion that we have a good opportunity to win this case on
appeal. If we do, we will have a new trial. At the new trial I
am going to hire another expert to testify about the bullets.

I also believe that your son is not guilty of killing anyone.
I will continue to do everything I know how to do to protect

him. I'm sorry that I missed your call when you called the other day, and I am certainly glad that you wrote to me to tell me about it. Please feel free to continue to contact me whenever you need to.

Sincerely, Sheldon Perhacs

Ray's heart broke at what he read between the lines of his letters—his mom calling Perhacs and writing him and asking him to protect her baby. What Ray didn't know at the time was that she was also sending Perhacs money orders for twenty-five dollars every time she wrote, pleading and begging him for help. *Here is all my money—save my son.* Did he laugh at those little money orders? Twenty-five dollars was nothing to a man who ate a thousand dollars for breakfast. But twenty-five dollars might as well have been a hundred thousand to Ray's mom. Perhacs didn't know what it meant to have just enough to make it through a month without a penny to spare. An extra ten dollars needed for an emergency would mean you had no water or no electricity for a month, or maybe even longer than a month, because you had to pay a reconnect fee to turn it back on. When Ray found out, he knew why his mom had never told him about the money—he would have put an end to it, never understanding that she needed the comfort of knowing she was doing everything she could to save her son's life. He would have taken that comfort from her.

He knew his mom felt helpless. So did Ray.

They all felt helpless.

And at the time, Ray didn't want to think his attorney would take advantage of that helplessness. How could he? Perhacs

77

was his only chance. Ray didn't tell his mom that Perhacs had already told Ray he would handle the automatic appeal and then he was off his case, back to his thousand-dollar breakfasts. It was as if he was already planning to lose. Ray was just hoping he would have a change of heart. A man had called him during Ray's trial and said he was the killer. Maybe he would call again. Ray was hoping for a miracle but planning his escape.

Ray hugged his mom and Miss Mae goodbye. His mom promised to come with Lester next time, and Miss Mae seemed relieved.

Visiting days were every Friday at first. Lester had to take the day off work, but as soon as he was allowed, he made the seven-hour round-trip drive every Friday. Sometimes he worked the night shift on Thursday and still drove all day Friday. Ray used to worry about him falling asleep at the wheel, but Lester was always the first one at the prison waiting to get in. He brought his mom and Ray's mom, and the three of them were the only bit of light in the darkness. Then the visits were changed to once a month for death row. They didn't want to make it easy on families and friends.

During those early visits, Ray was so full of hatred and rage that it was all he could do to smile and chitchat. If they noticed something wrong, they never said, but every once in a while, Ray could see Lester watching him. Lester was his best friend, he knew Ray better than anyone, but Ray didn't think Lester could have known what he was thinking.

Ray had never felt such a darkness in him. He couldn't control his thoughts. Every hour of every day, he imagined how he would kill McGregor. His days and nights were spent watching. And listening. At visiting hours, he was memorizing the routines of the guards. There had to be a way out. A moment where he could sneak over a fence, hide in the back of a car, take off running. It wasn't logical, and he didn't have a plan—but he watched and he waited because there had to be a way to escape. There just had to be.

Wouldn't it be better if they killed him while he was trying to escape rather than killing him strapped to a chair? The only hesitation Ray had was that he didn't want people to think he had run because he was guilty. He wanted to prove his innocence more than anything else.

Ray wasn't a killer, but now, he wanted to kill. Inside, he was becoming the monster the world thought he was, and he was afraid Lester and his mom would see it, so he lied to them about how things were. *The food is fine. The guards are nice. The other inmates are quiet and keep to themselves.* Ray lied to them every week. *I'm sleeping just fine. I have everything I need.* He lied and he lied and then he lied some more.

The reality was they had to eat breakfast at 3:00 a.m., lunch at 10:00 a.m., and dinner at 2:00 p.m. And every night, Ray was hungry. Every day, he was hungry. Breakfast was some powdered eggs, a biscuit so hard you could bounce it off the floor, and a little spoonful of what was supposed to be jelly. They had a whole prison to feed, so the death row inmates had to eat early in the morning. At 2:45 a.m., the guards would start screaming, "Breakfast! Breakfast! Breakfast!" If Ray was lucky enough to have fallen asleep, he would bolt upright in the dark, thinking he was under attack. Lunch was some bland patty of an unknown meat substance. He heard it was horsemeat, but he hoped that was just a bad joke. Dinner was the same formless patty, but at night, it was called a cutlet. On Fridays, there was a soggy fish cutlet. There were canned beans or peas or some other vegetable in a watery liquid that smelled slightly of tin and mold and tasted metallic and bitter. Instant mashed potatoes that would turn into a dry powder in your mouth.

Ray was hungry every day. It was a physical hunger, yes, but it was also a mental hunger. He hungered for home, for his own bed and his family and his church, and for friends he could laugh with and sit with. He was hungry for his freedom. He was alone all day with a hunger so big it felt like he was falling with nothing to grab on to. Like when you lean back in a chair and have that moment of panic where you've gone too far and you have to jerk yourself upright so you flail about to try to save yourself. Ray had that panic of falling all day, every day.

He was hungry for his dignity. He was hungry to be a human again. He didn't want to be known as inmate Z468. He was Anthony Ray Hinton. People called him Ray. He used to love to laugh. He had a name and a life and a home, and he wanted it so bad the wanting had a taste. He wasn't going to survive at Holman. Eventually, he would hollow out so completely he would just disappear into a kind of nothingness. They were all trying to kill him, and he was going to escape. He had no other choice.

DEATH PENALTY FACTS

- Dr. Benjamin Rush, founder of the Pennsylvania Prison Society, challenged the belief that the death penalty serves as a deterrent. Rush believed that capital punishment had a "brutalization effect" and actually increased criminal conduct. He gained the support of Benjamin

Franklin and Philadelphia attorney general William Bradford, who would later become the U.S. attorney general. In 1794, Pennsylvania repealed the death penalty for all offenses except first degree murder. (Bohm, 1999; Randa, 1997; and Schabas, 1997)[15]

- Pennsylvania went on to become the first state to end public executions by moving them from outdoor public spaces into correctional facilities by 1834. Twelve years later, Michigan abolished the death penalty except in cases of treason. Rhode Island and Wisconsin followed, abolishing capital punishment in all instances. But even as some states began to reject the death penalty, some states dug in even more with legislation that made *more* crimes punishable by death, especially those committed by enslaved people.[16]

- By the end of the nineteenth century, Venezuela, Portugal, Netherlands, Costa Rica, Brazil, and Ecuador abolished the death penalty. (Bohm, 1999 and Schabas, 1997)[17]. Today, the Death Penalty Information Center (DPIC) reports that "More than 70 percent of the world's countries have abolished capital punishment in law or practice."

---

15 https://deathpenaltyinfo.org/facts-and-research/history-of-the-death-penalty/the-abolitionist-movement

16 Ibid.

17 R. Bohm, "Deathquest: An Introduction to the Theory and Practice of Capital Punishment in the United States," Anderson Publishing, 1999; W. Schabas "The Abolition of the Death Penalty in International Law," Cambridge University Press, second edition, 1997.

- The death penalty, with its disproportionate impact on Black men, is linked to a legacy of lynching in the U.S. In its report *Lynching in America*, the Equal Justice Institute (EJI) states that "Lynching became a vicious tool of racial control in America during the late nineteenth and early twentieth centuries—but it first emerged as a form of vigilante retribution used to enforce 'popular justice' on the Western frontier . . . Southern lynching took on an even more racialized character after the Civil War." The idea of lynching became a way to exploit false and destructive ideas about Blackness and whiteness . . . "The link between lynching and the image of African Americans as 'criminal' and 'dangerous' was sometimes explicit, such as when lynchings occurred in response to allegations of criminal behavior. In other cases, white mobs justified lynching as a preemptive strike against the threat of Black violent crime."[18]

- The Civil Rights Act of 1964, a signature legal achievement of the civil rights movement, contains provisions designed to eliminate discrimination in voting, education, and employment, but it does not address discrimination in criminal justice.[19] The Equal Justice Institute reports that the criminal justice system, with its tacit embrace of racist myths about the humanity of Black people, remains in large part unchanged since the advent of the civil rights movement of the 1950s and 1960s.

---

18 https://lynchinginamerica.eji.org/report/

19 Ibid.

- A study in California found that those convicted of killing white people were more than 3 times as likely to be sentenced to death as those convicted of killing Black people and more than 4 times more likely as those convicted of killing Latinx people. (Pierce & Radelet, Santa Clara Law Review, 2005)[20]

Perhacs's motion for a new trial was postponed for over six months, until finally, on July 31, 1987, it was denied. It was exactly two years to the day that he had gotten arrested.

In Alabama at that time, you had forty-two days to file a notice of appeal and another twenty-eight days to file a brief. Did Ray find this out because Perhacs came to death row to visit with him and talk about a strategy for his appeal? Nope. He found this out by listening to the other death row inmates talking about their appeals.

It was like a legal class going on all day long, and while Ray still wasn't speaking, he did listen to the other inmates talking to each other.

"Man, you got to call Bryan Stevenson. He'll get you a lawyer in here."

"Bryan Stevenson sent his lawyer from up in Ohio. And another guy came from D.C."

"You have to tell him to read your transcript and see if they prejudiced the jury."

"Tell him about the guy who lied."

It went on all day, and Ray could hear the other inmates arguing case law with each other and talking about their appeals.

---

20 https://deathpenaltyinfo.org/documents/FactSheet.pdf

He learned that Alabama had just started electrocuting people again in 1983 after taking a break for eighteen years. Now people were afraid they were going to start giving out dates to everyone who had been there for a while and who didn't have an attorney trying to stop the State.

"He's got a bunch of lawyers helping him out. A whole resource center."

"I heard he's watching every single person on the row—tracking everybody. He's like Santa Claus, and he's gonna know if you are naughty or nice."

All day long, Ray heard the name Bryan Stevenson, but he didn't care about Bryan Stevenson. He cared about Perhacs and what he was doing for Ray's case. He had an attorney, and for that, he was grateful. It sounded like a lot of the guys were waiting for one to magically show up from the good graces of this one attorney named Stevenson. Ray didn't believe in God, and he sure didn't believe in Santa Claus. And he didn't ask any questions, because one thing he had learned from his trial was that if you said anything, people would lie about it if it helped their cases out. Ray didn't trust the other inmates. He didn't trust the guards. He didn't even trust Perhacs, but he was better than nothing. If Ray had to ask the guards for something, he wrote it down on the inmate stationery and handed it to them. He didn't know if they thought he was dumb or what, but they knew he spoke when he had his visits. Ray figured they were happy he didn't speak—it was one less inmate they had to deal with.

The guards brought him to the shower every other day, sometimes at 6:00 p.m.

Other times it would be at midnight.

There was no schedule. A guard walked in front of him, and a guard walked behind him. His hands were cuffed for the first three months, and after that he could go to the shower without being cuffed. There was no privacy in the shower, and there were always two guys showering at once and two guards watching. The water would be scalding hot or icy cold—it just depended on the day, or maybe what the guards felt like doing to entertain themselves. The prisoners had to soap up and get out fast, in under two minutes. The guards watched them the whole time—even the female guards. It was humiliating. They were like farm animals being hosed off outside the barn.

Once a day, they were brought out to individual cages in the yard that they could exercise in, or pace back and forth. Nobody had to "walk" as the guards called it, and a lot of guys just stayed in their cells. They didn't want to change or shower or exercise. Ray always took his fifteen or twenty minutes outside. He was looking for an escape. He could see the prison parking lot from his cage on the yard and the road that led away from Holman. He just needed to get to it. Every moment of every day, Ray was watching for a weakness in the system—despite what the prosecutors had said, he couldn't scale a fifteen-foot razor-wire fence. And certainly not one with guards and guns trained on it. He thought about digging a tunnel. There were rats and roaches that crawled in and out of his cell through a little vent near the ceiling. If they could get in, Ray thought, then he should be able to get out. He stared at that vent every day. There was always something lurking there—always an antenna or a whisker peeking through. Every night, he could hear the rats scratching and scurrying across the floors. He imagined the roaches swarming the walls at night and hiding back in the vent during the day to watch him. He was the trapped insect. Those roaches had more freedom than Ray did.

The sounds at night were like being in the middle of a horror movie—creatures crawling around, men moaning or screaming or crying. Everyone cried at night. One person would stop and another would start. It was the only time you could cry anonymously. Ray blocked out the sound. He didn't care about anyone's tears or their screams. Sometimes there was laughter—maniacal laughter—and that was the most frightening. There was no real laughter on death row. Those that could sleep yelled out in their dreams, as if they were being chased. Sometimes they cursed. Ray never slept more than fifteen minutes at a stretch ever in those first months and years. It makes people crazy to never sleep. It made them go to a place where there was no light, and no hope, and no dreams, and no chance for redemption. It made him think of shadows and demons and death and revenge and of killing before you can be killed.

Death and ghosts were everywhere. The row was haunted by remorse and regret and so much death. Freedom was a ghost that haunted them all on the row, those who had committed crimes, and those who hadn't—but most of all they were haunted by a past they could not go back and change. Loss and grief and a cold madness that defied words floated in the grime and filth that they were all coated in. Hell was real, and it had an address and a name.

Death Row, Holman Prison. Where love and hope went to die.

In 1988, the Court of Criminal Appeals affirmed his conviction. Ray didn't hear from Perhacs, but he got a copy of his appeal and the court's response. There were five issues Perhacs raised in his appeal. He said Judge Garrett made an error in

86

combining the two capital cases and not granting his motion to sever. He also said that there were two more errors when there were no test bullets entered into evidence. Finally, he said that the court never proved Ray was linked to the two murders, because they had no direct evidence he was there, and finally, that they should have been allowed to submit the polygraph test into evidence. The Court of Criminal Appeals disagreed with everything. Perhacs sent Ray a letter in April 1989. He was appealing his case to the Alabama Supreme Court.

At that point, Ray had been on death row for over two years.

April 11, 1989

Mr. Anthony Ray Hinton, #Z468 Holman Unit #37
Atmore, Alabama 36506
RE: Your case

Dear Anthony:

I presented oral argument for you to the Alabama Supreme Court yesterday. I got the impression that they were interested in the argument that I made, and I think we've got a pretty good opportunity to reverse your convictions to get a new trial. The court has ordered that additional brief be filed, and that will require approximately 2 weeks. After that they will take the case for their consideration. I'm unable to tell you exactly when to expect an opinion from them, but I've got a good feeling about this case. If the convictions are overturned, then we will have to prepare to defend these cases again. We will also have to prepare to defend the Quincy's cases. I've got a number of ideas about some

*things that we will do that will be new to each of the cases.
All of the cases continue to have very serious legal problems
within them, and I expect to take advantage of every legal
opportunity that is presented to us.*

*One of the things that I think we will have to do is hire
another expert. Even though our expert was willing to help
us, I don't think he was too persuasive with the jury. I thought
our presentation to the jury with Mr. Payne was excellent, but
he crumbled under their cross-examination. There really are a
lot of other things that we can do in addition to getting a new
expert.*

*If the Supreme Court does not order a new trial to you,
then I still think that we've got an excellent opportunity
to appeal this case to the United States Supreme Court.
The appeal I would take to the U.S. Supreme Court is not
financed or paid for by anybody.*

*Someone in your family would have to find a way to pay
some attorney's fees. Your case is so unique that I think the
U.S. Supreme Court would listen to your appeal. I really think
that sooner or later we are going to win these cases.*

Contact me if you have any questions.

Sincerely, Sheldon Perhacs

Ray read the letter at least five times. He did have a question. He had many questions. Why didn't Perhacs do all these "other things" the first time around? And what about Ray's innocence? Why didn't his appeal say anything about the fact that they had the wrong guy? The U.S. Supreme Court? Yeah, right. And he knew nobody in his family had any money to give him.

Ray had to hope that the Alabama Supreme Court ruled soon and ordered a new trial. He still hadn't found a way to escape, and he still wasn't ready to take his own life.

Ray wanted to prove he was innocent.

But he didn't know how much more he could take. He had to get out of Holman.

One way or another.

Chapter Ten

PAID IN FULL

"The death penalty is not about whether people deserve to die for the crimes they commit. The real question of capital punishment in this country is, Do we deserve to kill?"

—**Bryan Stevenson**, *Just Mercy: A Story of Justice and Redemption*

Ray didn't even realize they had executed Wayne Ritter until the middle of the night on August 28, 1987. There was the sound of a generator kicking on and then hissing and popping, and the lights in the hall outside his cell flickered on and off. And then through the night, the smell came. Ray couldn't explain what death smelled like, but it burned his nose and stung his throat and made his eyes water and his stomach turn over. He spent the next day dry heaving, his stomach retching and twisting. All up and down the row, he could hear men blowing their noses, trying to get the smell away. There was no real ventilation or air circulation, so the smell of death seemed to settle into his hair and in his throat and mouth. He rubbed at his eyes until they were red and gritty. Ray heard one of the guys complain to a guard about the smell.

"You'll get used to it." The guard laughed. "Next year or one of these days, somebody's going to be smelling you just the same. What do you think you gonna smell like to everyone? Not too good." The guard laughed again, and Ray felt his stomach turn over and heave as he ran to the toilet. The nightmare that was death row only got worse.

Ray wanted to ask how long Ritter had been there. Did they kill people every week? Every month? He wanted to know if Ritter knew they were killing him that day, but Ray still wasn't talking to anyone. He didn't know when they would come for him. Could they come kill him even though he was on appeal? If Perhacs failed, would they come take him right away—pull him from his cell in the middle of the night and strap him to the electric chair without warning? Ray couldn't stop his mind from racing and imagining what it would feel like to be sitting in that chair, and the fear, like a ton of bricks, crushed his chest until he thought he would stop breathing. Everything in him was fighting to run, but there was nowhere to go. It was like when you have a dream where you open your mouth to scream but no sound comes out and you stand there, mouth open and helpless, as danger descends. He wondered if he could get a gun from a guard on his way to the shower and then shoot his way out. Would that be a better way to die?

Ray spent months thinking about Ritter. He wondered if he had cried or pleaded for his life. Had he been guilty or innocent? Ray had never thought about the death penalty too much before being on death row. At trial, McGregor had asked Ray what he thought the appropriate sentence would be for someone who did what he was accused of doing, and he had said the death penalty would be appropriate. But was it? Who was he to say who was worthy of life or death? How could he or anyone know if someone was guilty or innocent? What happened to Ritter seemed like murder, and how was it okay to murder someone for murdering someone? Ray heard some guys say that after an execution, the cause of death listed on the death certificate was homicide. He didn't know if this was true or not. How could it be true? The thoughts swirled in his head all day and all night while he waited to see who the guards would come for next.

They started practicing a couple of months before the next execution. They called themselves the Execution Team, but everyone knew what they really were—the Death Squad. The Death Squad would line up, twelve of them in all, and march solemnly down the row. One guard would pretend to be the inmate, and the other would lead him to the holding cell that prisoners stayed in before being executed. The death chamber was only about thirty feet or so from Ray's cell. There was a guy a little younger than Ray in the cell below. Ray had never talked to him, but he knew his name was Michael Lindsey, and Ray knew Lindsey was the next to be executed. In the month leading up to his execution, Lindsey cried every day.

Ray had never heard anyone cry like that before; he remained silent. Michael Lindsey cried as the Death Squad practiced marching in front of his cell, and he cried as they went into the death chamber and turned the generator on to test Yellow Mama—that was the chair's nickname. He cried as the lights flickered, and he cried at night when the lights went out. The guards practiced their ritual for killing him, and then they would ask him how he was doing and did he need anything—as if they weren't rehearsing his murder. On the Monday before his execution, Ray could hear him begging and pleading with a guy named Jesse who had just started something called Project Hope to fight the death penalty from within Holman. Jesse had no power. He was on death row too. But Michael Lindsey begged him to save his life. It was heartbreaking and painful.

In the days leading up to your execution, you were allowed to have visitors all day each day. You were allowed to hug them and hold their hands—things you weren't allowed to do on regular visits. In nearly eight years on death row, Michael Lindsey never had a visitor. He was twenty-eight years old when the Death Squad came for him in May 1989.

He had been convicted of murdering a woman and stealing her Christmas presents. Ray thought about him crying and begging someone to save his life in those last days—and what it felt like for Lindsey to know there was nobody to save him, that the guards who were suddenly being so nice to him were going to be the same people who helped to kill him. He was only five years younger than Ray. He was healthy. A jury had recommended life in prison, but his judge had overruled that jury recommendation and sentenced him to death. Judges could do that in Alabama. Lindsey had been on death row for almost eight years. It was hard not to do the math—every inmate did the math when someone was executed—comparing how long the person killed had been there compared to how long you had been there.

Ray learned that they gave you an execution date around a month before you were executed. A month to feel terror. A month to beg and plead for your life. He didn't want to spend his last month on this earth crying and begging for his life. He didn't want to count down to his death. It was hard not to know when the Death Squad would come for you, but Ray thought it was even harder for the guys who knew.

Michael Lindsey had no last words. On Thursday night when they took him to the death chamber, Ray could hear him crying. They all could. He had no visitors in the days and hours before his death. He was completely alone. Shortly before midnight, when the inmates knew he was being strapped into that chair, they began to make some noise. Up and down the row, men began banging on the bars and doors of their cells. Ray heard some men yell, "Murderers!" to the guards. Some men screamed. Others called out Michael's name. Others just roared and growled like feral animals. Ray made a fist, and slammed it against the door of his cell as loud and as long as he could—until his hand was red and raw. The noise was intense, and you could hear guys yelling from general population as well. Ray didn't know Michael Lindsey, but he wanted him to know he wasn't alone. He wanted him to know that he saw him and knew him and his life meant something and so did his death. The inmates yelled until the lights stopped flickering and the generator that powered the electric chair turned off. Ray kept banging on his bars, and then he got in his bunk and pulled the blanket over his head and wept. He cried for a man who had to die alone, and he cried for whoever was next to die. He didn't want to see any more deaths. He didn't want to look at the guards tomorrow and wonder which one of them had done what to Michael as they brought him his food. He didn't want to live next to the death chamber, but there was nowhere to go. He would stay silent until he was set free.

Ray started to think about what must have driven Lindsey to steal Christmas presents, and he thought about his own family. They never had many Christmas presents, but he never felt like he was missing anything. Christmas had always been about love and celebrating the birth of Christ and family and good food and laughter. As crowded as his home was, it was fun and freedom, and he wanted nothing more than to be a kid again living in Praco and playing ball and roaming the hills and woods with Lester. He wanted open space, the smell of fresh-cut grass. He wanted to know that somewhere, somehow, there was a place where the sun shined and death didn't come for you at midnight and put a bag over your head. He closed his eyes and tried to sleep, but all Ray heard was Michael Lindsey begging somebody, anybody, to save him.

A few weeks after Lindsey was killed, another inmate, Dunkins, was given an execution date. Ray listened to the talk on the row. Dunkins was also twenty-eight. Everyone believed he had significant developmental disabilities and nobody thought he should be put to death. Alabama seemed to be making up for lost time, because another guy, Richardson, also got an execution date. Dunkins's was going to be in July '89, and Richardson's in August. It seemed like they were planning on executing one man per month now, and the row was tense and quiet. Right after Lindsey was killed, the heat had started up, and it seemed to get worse every day. No air circulated on the row, so it felt like sitting in a sauna all day and all night. Ray's fingers were wet and puckered like he'd been in water too long; that's how humid it was. He wanted to swim in cool water, and he was just imagining sitting in a cool stream when a guard came to his cell and opened the door.

"468!"

Ray just looked at him.

"468 . . . You got mail."

Ray didn't respond. He was Anthony Ray Hinton. People

called him Ray. He wasn't a number, and he wasn't going to speak.

"Still not speaking? You not dumb. I saw you last visit, talking and carrying on with your people."

Ray just looked down.

"You want this mail? It's a legal letter," he said. "You want it, you'd better say so."

Ray looked at the envelope in his hand. He could see LAW OFFICES OF SHELDON PERHACS stamped on it. This could be the answer he had been waiting on from the Alabama Supreme Court. His freedom! He could feel the hope rise up in him. Maybe they had caught the guy who did it, or maybe they were going to give him a new trial and a better expert, or maybe they had found out that he couldn't have been in two places at once, or maybe Reggie admitted to lying. He could feel the hope well up in him so big it even surprised him. Ray smiled at the guard. He didn't mean to, but it just happened.

"Well, that's something, then. At least you're not just scowling at the ground. You got to learn to cooperate around here, and things will get easier," the guard said. "You'd best be getting a better attitude if you want more privileges."

He didn't want more privileges, he wanted freedom. He wanted to get away from people who fed you one day and killed you the next. He had to get away from the smell of death and the heat of being in a small box twenty-three hours a day.

He took a deep breath and held out his hand. Ray and the guard both knew he had to give Ray legal mail, and the guard wasn't allowed to read it first either.

"Here you go." He handed Ray the letter. "And take a shower tonight. You stink."

Ray kept his head down until the guard left. He could have just slipped the mail through the slot, but he'd wanted to mess with Ray. Ray sat down on the edge of the bed and held the letter up in front of his face. His hands were shaking.

June 19, 1989

Mr. Anthony Ray Hinton, #Z468 Holman Unit #37
Atmore, Alabama 36506
RE: Your appeal to the Alabama Supreme Court

Dear Anthony:

Although I have not received the opinion as of yet, my office received a phone call from the clerk of the Supreme Court on Friday afternoon. The clerk reported to our office that our appeal to obtain new trials was denied.

So they had lost. But Perhacs went on to say there was still one more chance, if they acted fast. Well, if *someone* did, and it wasn't necessarily going to be Perhacs:

The appointment of me as your attorney of record does not continue from this point forward. In order for you to petition the U.S. Supreme Court for a review, you will have to hire an attorney. There is no requirement that you hire me, and there is no requirement that the federal government appoint an attorney to represent you. I will be more than happy to handle the appeal of your case from this point to the U.S. Supreme Court, but my fee to do that would be $15,000.00. *The conditions for the payment of the fee are*

97

difficult; it would be my requirement that the entire fee be paid immediately in order for me to begin the appellate process. *Please contact your family instantly and contact me immediately with your decision about what it is you would like to do.*

Sincerely, Sheldon Perhacs

Ray was almost motionless for the next twenty-four hours. They came for him to take a shower, but he wouldn't respond or get up off the bed, and eventually, they gave up and moved on to the next guy. Once again, it came down to money. Was Perhacs shaking him down? Shaking down his family? Ray was on death row for supposedly killing people so he could steal some money—where did he think Ray had $15,000 hiding? Ray called his office and spoke to his secretary.

"Can't your mom mortgage her house?" she asked. "That's what he's thinking will have to happen."

"Tell him thanks for everything," Ray said.

"That's it, then?" she asked.

"That's it. If he won't go on without money, then we're done. I don't have money. My family don't have money. I'm not going to let my mom mortgage her house."

He heard her sigh and say she would give Perhacs the message, and he'd get a message to the prison or come to see Ray to talk about it.

Ray knew he wouldn't see him again.

When his mom and Lester came at the end of that week to visit, he pulled Lester aside so they could talk for a minute away from their moms.

"Listen," Ray said. "Listen quick. Perhacs is done. My appeal is done. No matter what Perhacs says if he calls you, don't let him get to my mother. He wants her to mortgage her house, and that's just him still trying to shake us down for money. It's over."

Lester shook his head. "It can't be over. There's got to be something—"

"Listen," Ray interrupted him. "When they give me a date, that's it. I don't want you watching or anyone watching me die. You bring them for a visit, and then you take them to a hotel nearby to spend the night."

He could see Lester shaking his head.

"When I'm gone—it will be a little after midnight, but don't wake her up; wait until morning—then you tell her, 'He's gone and he said he loves you.'"

Lester put his hands up over his face. "I can't tell her that you're gone. I can't."

"You're going to have to, and I'm sorry about that. I am." He took a deep breath. "You remind her of what she's always said: 'There's a time to live and a time to die.' You remind her. You keep saying it to her. You tell her that I love her, and that I wasn't scared, and that all of us is going to have to leave this world at some point and it was just my time. You tell her that when her time comes, I'm going to have some of her favorite food waiting, and I'll have a nice place for her to stay, and I'll be waiting."

Lester was crying and wiping at his eyes.

"You going to have to bring her own words back on her, over and over again. That's the only thing that will help her. Do you understand? You tell her what she's always said. You tell her God makes no mistakes. Everything happens for a reason. And you play that back to her over and over no matter how she be crying and carrying on. Tell her, God come got what was his, and there's a time to live and a time to die. That's what she taught me. That's what she's got to remember."

"Why do I have to do it? Can't your sisters or one of your brothers?" Lester's face had a pain in it Ray had never seen before, and its broke Ray's heart to know that he was the cause.

"You're my brother, Lester. You're the best, closest family I have. Do you see anyone else here on visiting day? Do you see a line of my sisters and brothers waiting to see me? You're the only one to do this for me, and she'll listen to you. She'll need you more than ever. Promise me you'll look after her. Promise me you'll comfort her. It's going to break her heart, but you tell her God needed me and brought me home. Tell her that we all have a season for living and a season for dying. Tell her that. Tell her it was just my time and you tell her I died with joy in my heart and I wasn't afraid, and I had God by my side."

He grabbed Lester's arm. "You lie to her, Lester. You lie to her until she's at peace, you understand?"

"I'm not going to let them kill you."

"Just promise me."

"We're going to find a way to get you out of here. I'm going to find someone else to help you. Someone besides Perhacs."

"You just keep him from Mama's house, you understand?"

Lester nodded, but he had a stubborn look about him that Ray recognized from when they were kids.

"There's a time for living and a time for dying," Ray said. "It's true."

"It ain't true today."

"It's true today, Lester. It's always true in this place."

They killed Horace Dunkins on July 14. The inmates banged against the bars and the lights flickered and then they stopped.

And then ten minutes later, the generator went back on and the lights flickered again.

Human error, they called it. He had to be electrocuted twice over nineteen minutes because the guards hooked up the cables wrong.

Herbert Richardson was executed a month later. He was a Vietnam veteran, a man who had served his country, and now his country saw fit to end his life. He asked to be blindfolded before he was brought in so he couldn't see the death chamber, or the people watching him, or anything. Ray and the other prisoners banged on the bars for Dunkins and for Richardson, just so they both knew they weren't alone.

Ray found out after the execution that Richardson wasn't alone. A young attorney named Bryan Stevenson had sat with him all day and stayed with him through the end, even as he tried to get the execution stayed. Ray heard the other inmates talking about it. He wondered again who this guy was and what it must be like for him to have to watch his clients die.

Ray spent his days waiting to hear when they would come to give him his death date and his nights reliving every moment of his trial. He thought of things he could have said. Witnesses Perhacs could have called. *Why didn't he bring up my family to tell the jury why I shouldn't be killed? Why not bring up Lester? The people from church? My neighbors?* He thought about McGregor, but some of his hate had dulled to a kind of listless apathy. He was the devil, but who was he to do anything about the devil? His Bible had been under his bed for almost three years.

Ray hadn't spoken to anyone. He hadn't gotten to know the

guards or any other inmates except through what he overheard. He was completely alone. Even the miserable Perhacs was gone. That was it. He was going to die an innocent man, and nobody would know but him, Lester, and his mom.

"Hinton!" The guard yelled his name and startled him up out of the bed.

Ray heard the door open. Was this it? Were they giving him a death date? Taking him to the holding cell? Was it his time to be killed?

He clenched his fists. He wasn't going to willingly walk to his death. He was innocent. He didn't deserve to be electrocuted. *No one did. No one deserved to die like this.* They were all children of God. He wanted to reach his hand under the bed and pull out his Bible. Why had he left God? Why had he turned his back on his comfort? Ray needed him now. He was going to have his head shaved and a bag thrown over his face, and he wasn't going to be able to look anyone in the eyes so they could see that he faced his death an innocent man.

It was time to fight. He would grab the guard's gun. He would make a run for it. He wanted to die a free man. He wanted to die on his terms. His mind was racing, and his heart was pounding. Adrenaline shot through his veins. He had to make his move. It was time. He couldn't be led like a lamb to slaughter. He couldn't. This was not God's will for him. This was not why he was born into this life. He was Anthony Ray Hinton. People called him Ray. This was wrong, and he was going to fight his death to the end.

He wanted to go home.

He needed to go home.

"Hinton! Legal visit!" The guard stood staring at Ray, his

hand on his gun. What had he seen in Ray's face? Ray had been seconds away from lunging at him.

Ray followed him up to the visiting area. There were no other inmates in the room. A solitary white woman, about his age, with short brown hair, sat at one of the tables.

She stood up and gave Ray a huge smile. Then she held out her hand for him to shake.

He just stared at her.

"Mr. Hinton, I'm Santha Sonenberg from Washington, D.C. I'm your new attorney."

Ray shook her hand, but he was sure his confusion showed.

She cocked her head to the side and gave him another smile. "Mr. Hinton, please sit down."

Ray sat.

"I'm going to file your writ of certiorari petition in the U.S. Supreme Court."

"I don't have any money."

She looked at him sharply. "I'm not asking you for money. No one expects you to pay any money."

"But my first attorney wanted $15,000 to file this writ thing. He wanted my mom to mortgage her house. That's not going to happen. I will die first."

Santha inhaled and exhaled loudly. "Okay. Let's take it one step at a time. There's no money involved. I will file the petition, and honestly, it's not likely that the U.S. Supreme Court is going to do anything; they typically don't. The certiorari petition is basically asking the Supreme Court to review the lower court's ruling. They don't grant a review all that often. But the actual petition asking them to review is not a big deal to prepare. We're going to handle it in the time frame needed. Then we're going to investigate and do what's called a Rule 32 petition back in the circuit court in Jefferson County."

Ray just stared at her. He didn't understand much of what she was saying, but she was there. She was going to investigate. She was going to file some new stuff.

"I want you to know I'm innocent," he said. "I didn't kill anyone. I hope you can believe me."

"I believe you." She took a deep breath.

"In my transcripts, you'll see that Perhacs got a phone call from someone who claimed he was the real killer. My mom got a call too. You have to find a way to trace that number. Nobody found him. He gave a fake name. We need to find him. You need to find him."

Santha nodded like she knew all about it. "We're going to investigate everything. But first I'm going to ask you a lot of questions—about your life, your family, what it was like growing up, the trial, your relationships, everything that matters. I'm going to review the trial transcript and Perhacs's records. I'm going to look at all the evidence, and we're going to see what we can do, okay? I want you to stay strong. Are you doing okay here?"

"Can they put me to death while you are investigating and we're appealing?" He held his breath.

"No, Mr. Hinton. They can't put you to death while your case is in the courts."

He put his head down on the table and took a few breaths. When he lifted his head back up, he knew he had tears in his eyes, but Santha didn't say anything about that.

"I'm going to need your help. We're going to have to work together on this. Do I have your permission to represent you?"

She was staring at Ray intently. "Mr. Hinton, are you going to be okay?"

He smiled at her. "Yes, you have my permission, but call me Ray."

"Okay, Ray. Let's get to work."

"Just one more thing," he asked. "How did you become my attorney? Did Lester call you?"

She shook her head. "I'm sorry, I don't know who Lester is."

"How are you here?" Ray asked. "How did you know about me?"

Santha Sonenberg smiled.

"Bryan Stevenson sent me. He knows about everyone."

Chapter Eleven

WAITING TO DIE IS NO WAY TO LIVE

"To take a life when life has been lost is revenge, not justice."

—Archbishop Desmond Tutu

The U.S. Supreme Court denied Ray's petition on November 13, 1989.

There was no explanation.

Four days later, Arthur Julius was executed.

Ray banged on the bars of his cell with the others until about ten minutes after midnight, and then the guards came through and angrily told them to quiet down. "He heard you," one of them said. "Everyone heard you."

Ray didn't know Arthur or if he had done it or not, but he assumed he had. Ray was under no illusion that everyone on death row was innocent, but he also knew that not everyone was guilty.

Ray knew Santha was working on his case, but he still wasn't speaking to anyone, and even though he didn't think they were going to come for him in the night and strap him to that terrible yellow chair, he still had fear and anxiety that never went away. Apart from his visits with Lester and the moms, Ray spent his time lying on his bunk, staring at the ceiling. He had no energy to eat, talk, or even clean his cell. What was the point? He didn't want to make a home out of hell. He didn't want to make it okay that they had him there.

McGregor had called him *Mr. Sneak. Mr. Robber. Mr. Executioner.* Why had he decided Ray was so evil he had to make it his personal mission to bend and twist the truth in ways that defied logic and common sense? Ray wanted to ask him: *Why me?* Or could it have been any Black man? Every second of his arrest and his trial ran like a loop in his head. Ray worried that he would lose it before his next appeal even got started. McGregor was everything he accused Ray of being. *He* was the executioner. *He* was the liar and the sneak and the robber, because he had robbed Ray of his life. His exact words to the jury played over and over in Ray's head. "Look at the evidence, take the time to," he had said to them, "and I'm going to ask you to find the truth. Find the truth in this case. Look at the evidence. Remember the testimony. You find the truth, and you do justice."

Those sentences played in an endless loop, like a song that just keeps starting over from the beginning. *McGregor deserves to die, not me. He is the guilty one. He is the murderer.* He should be the one who felt afraid every time he walked to the shower, or went outside with killers, or smelled the burning flesh of dying men. He should be condemned. McGregor was not innocent.

It had to be well after midnight when Ray heard the first sob. There were always men yelling and moaning and crying—every single night. But it had been strangely quiet for about twenty minutes, so when he heard the noise, it jolted him. He had gotten used to tuning out the endless sounds of pain on death row. It was just background noise and not any of his business.

But there was something about that first sob.

It was a sound low and guttural, almost more growl than cry. Then a guard walked past his cell door. Ray could see the silhouette of his legs from the light in the corridor.

There was another sob and a catch, like someone was trying to hold it in. The sound was close to him. It had to be the guy next to him or one cell over. Ray couldn't tell. The sobbing got a bit louder, and Ray tried to tune it out, go back to McGregor and Reggie and Perhacs and Judge Garrett.

They should have tried harder to find the guy who called Perhacs to say he was the killer. It was all too much work to investigate the real killer, so Ray could just hear McGregor: *Let's just make it so this guy did it, and we can say good night to these cases and the victims' families will feel better.* Who was that guy who called in? Was he really the killer or just some weirdo who wanted to get into the action on a trial that was in all the papers? The guy had called Ray's mom also, and Perhacs's home and office. It seemed like a lot of effort for a guy who wasn't serious. Ray figured he was surprised when no one seemed to care that they had the wrong guy. Maybe he even felt bad for Ray. Ray imagined this guy coming to the prison or going to the media—to confess and take his place on death row, to save his soul. Ray played out the whole scenario in his head—the guy finding God and needing to confess and repent—maybe he would call McGregor next time or the judge . . . Suddenly, he heard a voice.

"Oh my God . . . please help me. I can't take it. I just can't take it anymore."

Ray snapped out of his imaginings and listened to the man crying. The sobbing got deeper. Heavier. Did he really believe God was going to help him? There was no God in this place. There was no choice but to take it until you couldn't take it anymore or they killed you. God may sit high, but he wasn't looking low. He didn't see them there, in hell. There was no light in this dark place, so there was no God and no help and no hope.

Ray said all this in his head, but he couldn't drown out the sound of his neighbor's crying. The man's crying was so low and deep it seemed to pound inside his chest like when someone has the bass turned way up on their stereo. Ray tried harder to block it out. It wasn't his problem. It was every man for himself on the row, and Ray didn't trust anyone. He would never trust anyone again. People lied. People sold you for money. People didn't care about the truth, so he didn't care about people. The only people for Ray were the ones who showed up every week to visit. Lester and the moms.

Ray sat up out of bed and began pacing the few feet he had room to walk around in in his cage. It was steps from his toilet to his cell door.

One. Two. Three. Four. Five.

He counted them out in his head and then turned around and counted them again as he walked to the back of his cell. Back and forth. He couldn't lie there while the man sobbed like an animal who had his foot caught in a trap.

"God help me. Oh God. I can't take it. I can't, I can't, I can't . . ." The man was crying and moaning, and Ray could do nothing but count and walk and turn and count and walk and turn. Over and over again.

One. Two. Three. Four. Five.

Ray thought about his mom. He had called her earlier that day, and they had gotten to talk for a few minutes. She was cooking up a big dinner for Lester when Ray called. They were having a celebration dinner.

"What are you celebrating?" Ray had asked.

"Lester's getting married."

"Mama, you're crazy." Ray had laughed at her. If Lester was getting married, he would have told Ray himself. Unless he'd just met the girl since last week when he was there for a visit. Nobody had said anything.

"It's true," she'd said. "He's getting married to Sylvia—you know, that good girl from church whose husband died in a fire." It hadn't surprised Ray that his best friend had found a girlfriend who happened to have the same name as the woman Ray had been seeing. But marriage?

"Mama, you got to stop gossiping. You don't know what you're talking about." He'd laughed. Lester would have told him.

But she'd insisted, so Ray had changed the subject to their next visit.

"Now, you try to sneak me some pie up in here. Bring some extra for the guards. Try to bribe them with some peach pie." She just laughed every time he'd said that. His mom would no sooner break the law than she would grow two heads. "Now, I'm going to hang up because these collect calls are expensive. I'll see you Friday. I love you."

"I love you too, baby."

Ray had hung up the phone and put Lester getting married out of his mind. But now, with nothing to do but pace and listen to the sorrow of another man, he had to admit it hurt. It hurt that Lester hadn't told him himself, but Ray understood why he wouldn't want to talk to Ray about dating and falling in love and getting married while Ray was stuck on death row. What really hurt was the stabbing sensation Ray felt at the idea that he might die before he got the chance to date again, or fall in love, or get married. Ray thought about his Sylvia, who he'd had to leave behind. And now Lester had a Sylvia. Lester's life was moving forward, like a life was meant to do. Things were supposed to change. Life was not supposed to be exactly the same every day. No human was supposed to spend every single day in a small box doing exactly the same thing as they did the day before and that they would do tomorrow. Ray knew why Lester didn't tell him he was getting married—he didn't want Ray to think about what he was missing. He didn't want Ray to hurt any more than he was already hurting.

No one can understand what freedom means until they don't have it. Ray would give anything right then to have a choice to make—any choice. *I think I'll go for a walk rather than go to bed right now. I think I'll have chicken for dinner. I think I'd like to take a drive and just see where I end up.* Ray was happy for Lester. Ray wanted nothing more than for Lester to be happy. He would be sorry to miss the wedding and sad not to be able to stand next to his best friend and be his best man. He had to get out of this place. He thought about the children he would never have if he didn't get off death row. He wanted a son to play baseball with someday. And basketball. He wanted to take him to Auburn games so he knew there was only one team in Alabama that mattered. Ray wanted to show him the woods, and the river, and the quiet beauty of a night spent in the country. He wanted to show him how to fish and teach him how to drive. He wanted to show him that anything was possible in this world if you only had faith.

He stopped pacing.

Faith. How could he teach anyone about faith when he didn't have it?

"Oh God. Help me, God . . ." The crying was intermittent now, and Ray realized he was holding his breath when it stopped and waiting for it to start again. He didn't know which was worse—the crying or the silence. Men killed themselves all the time in this prison.

He went back to pacing. This wasn't any of his business.

One. Two. Three. Four. Five.

He would wait for Lester to tell him about getting married. Ray didn't want to make him feel bad for finding love and happiness. That's what real friendship was all about. Or any relationship, for that matter. You wanted the other person's happiness as much as, or more than, your own. Lester deserved love. Hell, everyone deserved love.

The man started crying again, and Ray realized that he was crying too. He sat down on the edge of the bed, and wept silently for a man he didn't even know, who was most likely a killer, but who also wept in the dark, all alone, in a cage, in Atmore, Alabama. You didn't have to be on death row to feel all alone, and Ray knew there were people all over the world, at this exact moment, sitting on the edge of their beds and crying. Most days it seemed like there was more sadness than sense in the world. He sat there for a few more minutes, listening to the other man crying.

Lester had choices, and Ray was glad he was making them. He thought again about all the choices he didn't have and about freedom, and then the man stopped crying and there was a silence that was louder than any noise Ray had ever heard. What if this man killed himself that night and Ray did nothing? Wouldn't that be a choice?

Ray still had choices, and that knowledge rocked him. He still had some choices. He could choose to give up or to hang on. Hope was a choice. Faith was a choice. And more than anything else, love was a choice. Compassion was a choice.

"Hey!" He walked up to his cell door and yelled toward the crying man. "Are you all right over there?"

There was nothing but silence. Maybe he was too late. "Hey, you okay?" Ray asked again.

"No," he finally answered.

"Is something wrong? Do you need me to call for an officer or something?"

"No, he just left."

"Okay, then."

Ray stood at the bars. He didn't know what to say or what to do. It was weird to hear his own voice on the row. He only spoke during visits. The man didn't say anything else. Ray started to walk back to his bed, but then he thought about what his neighbor had been saying when he was sobbing. *Please help me. I can't take it anymore.*

He walked back up to the door. "Hey, man. Whatever it is, it's going to be all right. It's going to be okay."

It had to be another five minutes before the man spoke. "I just . . . I just got word . . . that my mom died."

Ray could hear him trying to hold back the tears as he talked. In that moment, his heart broke wide open and he wasn't a convicted killer on death row; he was Anthony Ray Hinton from Praco. People called him Ray. His mama called him Ray. He was his mama's son. "I'm sorry, man. I really am."

His neighbor didn't say anything back, and then Ray heard a guy yell from down below, "Sorry for your loss." And then another from the left yelled, "Sorry, man. Rest in peace." Nobody else was talking before that, but they had been listening too. They'd heard him crying. Ray didn't have to think about people all around the world sitting on the edge of their beds and crying when there were almost two hundred men all around him who didn't sleep, just like him. Who were in fear just like him. Who wept just like anyone. Who felt alone and afraid and without hope.

He had a choice to reach out to these men or to stay in the dark alone. Ray walked over to his bed and got on his hands and knees. He reached his arm under the bed and felt around through the dust and dirt until the tips of his fingers brushed against his Bible. It had been under there for too long. This man had lost his mom, but Ray still had his, and she wouldn't care for his Bible to be collecting filth. Even on death row, he could still be himself.

"Listen!" he yelled. "God may sit high, but he looks low. He's looking down here in the pit. He's sitting high, but he's looking low. You've got to believe it." Ray had to believe it too.

He heard an "Amen!" from somewhere on the row.

"It's a hard loss to bear. But your mom's looking down on you too."

"I know. Thanks."

Then Ray asked the man to tell him about his mom and he listened for the next two hours as his neighbor told story after story. His mom seemed a lot like Ray's mom. Tough, but full of love.

The man started crying again, but softer than he had at the beginning of the night.

Ray wondered why it was that the cries of another human being can touch in unexpected ways. Ray wasn't expecting to have his heart break that night. He wasn't expecting to end three years of silence. Ray believed he was born with the same gift from God that all are born with—the impulse to reach out and lessen the suffering of another human being. Each person had a choice whether to use this gift or not.

Ray didn't know his neighbor's story or what he had done or anything about him that made him different from Ray—he didn't even know if the guy was Black or white. But on the row, Ray realized, it didn't matter.

What Ray knew was that this man loved his mother just like Ray loved his mother. He could understand that pain.

"I'm sorry you lost your mom, but man, you got to look at this a different way. Now you have someone in heaven who's going to argue your case before God."

It was silent for a few moments, and then the most amazing thing happened. On a dark night, in what must surely be the most desolate and dehumanizing place on earth, a man laughed.

A real laugh.

And with that laughter, Ray realized that the State of Alabama could steal his future and his freedom, but they couldn't steal his soul or his humanity. And they most certainly couldn't steal his sense of humor. He missed his family. He missed Lester. But he knew that sometimes you have to make family where you find family, or you die in isolation. Ray wasn't ready to die. He wasn't going to make it that easy on them. He was going to find another way to do his time. Whatever time he had left.

He had a choice.

And it hit him: Spending your days waiting to die is no way to live.

Chapter Twelve

TEA WITH THE QUEEN

"Not many people have seen a real death warrant in person, let alone been issued one with their name on it. I remember the warden instructing security to escort us in restraints from our cells, one at a time, to a small office where we were surrounded by prison officials. The warden read aloud the information off the warrants, which included our names, our crimes, and the jury's verdict . . . I was handed the death warrant, a longer-than-usual sheet of paper with the golden seal of the State of Arkansas fixed on it. At the bottom, there was the signature of Gov. Asa Hutchinson.

"Death, one step closer. Tick, tick."

—Kenneth Williams[21]

Time runs differently in prison. Sometimes it passes as if in slow motion, every hour feeling like three, every day like a month, every month like a year—and every year a decade. In regular population, time is something to count down until a release date, crossing off each day happy to have gotten through it and thankful to be one day closer to leaving—to freedom. On death row, it's different. The countdown is toward execution, and when an inmate gets that date, time speeds up. It runs as if someone

---

21 www.themarshallproject.org/2017/04/06/my-execution-20-days-away#
.rrkVsNaxD

has pressed fast-forward, and every day feels like an hour, every hour feels like a minute, and every minute feels like a second.

In prison, time is a strange and fluid thing, but time on death row is even more warped.

Everyone, including Ray, knew there were only two ways to leave the row—dead on a gurney or set free by the law. He wasn't ready to leave on a gurney, so he started praying at night for his new attorney and for the truth to finally come out. He didn't just pray for his release, because that wasn't enough. Ray wanted the truth to come out. He wanted people to know that he was innocent. He wanted McGregor to apologize. He wanted the jury to know they had gotten it wrong and for other juries to learn from their mistakes. The only way that could happen was if he was found innocent. Ray was also a little suspicious. Growing up, he'd heard too many stories of folks praying for things in a general way and having it turn out badly for them when it seemed like their prayers were answered in a literal way. He knew a guy in the county jail who used to pray every day to get to leave C block. Everybody knew he wasn't going to leave before his trial, but he said he was praying and he knew God was going to answer his prayers. The next day, he was caught smoking, and when they turned over his cell looking for his stash, the guards found a weapon he had made out of broken plastic from his meal tray. He did leave C block, but only to go into solitary confinement.

So Ray said his prayers carefully. He prayed for Lester and their moms. He prayed for Lester's new wife, and he prayed for his church family, neighbors, his siblings, and his nieces. He prayed for Sid Smotherman, and for the families of John Davidson and Thomas Vason, the men who had been murdered. But mostly Ray prayed for the truth. *Truth* was a big, broad word, but he knew there was no gray area and no way to misinterpret his prayer. Ray prayed for God to reveal the truth—and whether that meant they proved him innocent or they caught the guy who really did it or Reggie confessed to lying, didn't matter. Ray knew that the truth would set him free. He read John 8:32 in his Bible: "Then you will know the truth, and the truth will set you free." He also read Mark 11:24. "What things so ever you desire when you pray, believe that you receive them, and you shall have them." If it was true that God could do everything but fail, then the truth had to be known. The truth had to set him free. If he believed it, it would happen. It had to.

Ray had gotten a few letters from Santha Sonenberg, so he knew she was investigating his case. He spoke to Santha on the phone, and she apologized for not being able to come visit again but told him she was busy preparing his Rule 20 petition, which was a petition for relief from convictions and sentences of death. A petition for relief asks the court to make a new and separate judgment; an appeal is like getting a second opinion, asking for a reconsideration of a judgment. Ray knew he had to pray and believe.

The State of Alabama gave Santha a deadline to file Ray's petition, and she would be sending Ray a copy when she filed it. Inmates were allowed to go to the law library once a week for an hour, and Ray had refused his time for the past three years, but now he went every week. They weren't allowed to bring any books back to their cells—all they were allowed were Bibles or other religious books—so for an hour every week, Ray would read about the law in Alabama. He learned what a capital conviction really was, and he read about aggravating and mitigating circumstances. He read about "judicial override"—even if a jury said life in prison, a judge in Alabama could override the jury and still send you to the electric chair. To Ray, it just seemed like another way to put an innocent man to death. He couldn't understand the point in having a jury if a judge could just go ahead and do whatever he wanted. How was that justice? Why was Alabama so hell-bent on putting people to death one way or another?

When he went back to his cell, Ray had questions. "Y'all heard of this judicial override business?" he yelled. He pointed out that it made no sense, and was automatically unfair. It still felt strange to be speaking, like being the new kid at school.

Several other voices yelled out in encouragement.

"It seems like it defeats the purpose of a jury if a judge can just do what he wants," he went on. "As if the cards aren't stacked against you enough already."

"Preach it, brother!" another voice yelled out. There was some laughter.

"I'm going to read up on it some more next week," Ray said. "Some of you should do the same."

A voice he hadn't heard earlier yelled out, "I'm here because of that judge overriding the jury. The jury said life."

"Me too," yelled another voice. "It's 'cause them judges got to get elected. That's all. They get more votes the more men they send to the death chair."

Ray stood at the front of his cell. It was weird to have a discussion when he couldn't see anybody and couldn't always tell who was talking. He was beginning to distinguish guys from their voices. Their accents.

"The police lied and said I took a dollar from the guy." It was the first voice again. "That's how I even got a capital case. I'm not saying what I did, or even if I did anything, but I'm just saying they lied and said I took one dollar. One dollar. That made it a capital case. And then when the jury said, 'Life,' the judge said, 'Nope . . . it's gonna be death.'"

The guy sounded choked up. "What's your name, man?" Ray yelled.

The man didn't answer for a few minutes, and the row got strangely quiet. Even though there were guys around him who had to know his name, it was his to tell or not to tell. You didn't speak for anyone on the row, and you didn't name names ever.

"My name's Ray," Ray said. "Anthony Ray Hinton, but folks call me Ray." There was silence. He rested his left cheek up against the mesh wire of his door. He could wait. They had nothing to do but wait. There was something in this guy's voice. He sounded alone. "I'm from Praco," Ray kept talking. "And proud to be the son of Buhlar Hinton, the best mother God ever sent down to this earth, who can make a pie like an angel and swat you like the devil if you try to eat it before she says so."

He heard a few guys laugh, but he didn't know if the guy whose name he was waiting on was one of them.

"My mom makes a pretty good pie herself," the man finally said. "My name is Henry." Henry didn't say his last name, and Ray didn't care to ask him. The guards called them by number or last name, rarely by first name. Ray would no sooner ask for a last name than he would ask him what someone was in for. Some things you never asked. If someone wanted to talk about it, that was one thing. But you never asked. And really, what did it matter? They were all protecting themselves and reaching out at the same time. What else could they do?

"Nice to meet you, Henry. And I hope someday we can sit together in the shade on a beautiful Fourth of July, drinking sweet tea while our mothers compete to see who can make us the best pie. I don't know about your mom, but mine loves a good competition."

Henry laughed. "Well, that would be something to see, Ray. You have no idea. That would really be something."

"I'm sorry about your case, Henry," Ray said. "That doesn't sound right. It doesn't sound right at all. I'm going to do some more research next week on this judge override. You should do the same."

He didn't say anything back, so Ray dropped it.

"You know they don't like it when we educate ourselves," he yelled out. "The South still isn't happy we ever learned to read."

"Preach it, brother!"

"Is that you, Jesse?" Ray hollered back.

"Last time I checked, it was. I'm still here. You still here, Wallace?"

"I'm still here!"

And up and down the row it went, guys calling out to each other cell by cell. Sometimes they asked by name; other times they just asked in general. "You still here?" And a different voice would yell back, "I'm still here!"

And with each voice, it got funnier and funnier. Ray started laughing. Each man who yelled that he was still here made him laugh harder. There they were in their cages. It shouldn't have been funny, but it was.

"We are all still here!" Ray yelled out one last time, and then he lay back on his bed. It was a good day when he could find a little bit of light.

Ray didn't hear from Henry again that day, but there was no need to push it. Maybe they'd become friends, maybe not.

He thought about Wallace. He had been yelling and laughing, and everyone knew he had an execution date in less than two weeks. It made Ray's stomach turn over a bit. Wallace and Jesse had started Project Hope, the inmate advocacy group to fight the death penalty. Ray didn't see how it was really going to change anything, but he knew it helped to feel like you were doing something. He knew they had gotten permission to meet up as a small group, and he was sure some guys just went to have another opportunity to get out of their cells. They were still only allowed less than an hour out of their cells every day. That and visiting day and law library was it. The warden only let a small group meet for Project Hope, and Ray hoped they didn't cause any trouble. If someone on the row caused trouble, it made a problem for everyone. The warden had no issue with locking them down all day or taking away their visits if anyone did anything. Ray was a nice guy to everyone, but he definitely wasn't going to let some fool stop his visits. Lester came every week, no matter what, and apart from those six hours with him and their moms, Ray had very few ways to keep himself occupied. He was reading his Bible again, but a man can't read only the Bible. It's like only having steak for dinner. You might love steak, but if you have it every day of the week, eventually you're going to get sick of it.

Ray read his Bible before Wallace was executed on July 13, 1990.

Wallace wore a purple ribbon and a sign that said EXECUTE JUSTICE, NOT PEOPLE.

They banged on the bars for Wallace Norrell Thomas. Some banged on the bars to protest the death penalty. Others banged on the bars just to have something to do or as a way to let off steam. Ray banged on the bars so Wallace would know that he mattered. That he was not alone. Ray figured everyone wanted to know they mattered to someone, anyone. He knew he mattered to his mom and Lester and Phoebe, and that was more than a lot of these guys had. A lot of guys came here and died here without ever getting a visit. A lot of them never had a parent who loved them.

A few weeks after Wallace was killed, Ray got a letter from Santha, a handwritten note, which was unusual.

Mon 8/6/90

Mr. Hinton—

Apologies for the delay in getting this to you & for such an informal note. As I mentioned, I'm ½-way to finishing the Rule 20 petition. I met with Bryan Stevenson this morning and we have many ideas for your case.

I'm sorry not to have been able to visit you today. Please know that it's only because I want to do the best job I can on writing your petition.

Stay strong & stay in touch! I'll be sending you a copy of the petition next week.

Best Wishes,
Santha

Ray read the letter over and over again. She had written her home number in the bottom-right corner of the letter in red ink. He appreciated that, and he looked forward to getting the petition, not only so he knew his appeal was moving forward but also so he could have something else to read. Anything to occupy his mind.

He couldn't understand why they weren't allowed to have books. He thought about Wallace and his group. What if he started a group? What could his group be about? What would help the guys not feel so alone? What could help them all escape this place for a bit?

Ray thought back to being in the coal mines. He never would have imagined it, but now he would give anything to be working there again. He had hated it at the time, but he remembered how he had escaped the misery of it. He had traveled in his mind. He closed his eyes and thought about where he would go if he were off death row.

He was walking out the front door of the prison. There was a plane waiting; it was parked right in the parking lot between the two fences. A private jet. It was white, and inside, it had soft leather seats the color of butter. Ray sat down, and immediately, a beautiful flight attendant appeared. She had dark skin and red lips and a smile so big he thought he would die right then and there.

"Mr. Hinton, can I get you something to drink? Champagne, perhaps?"

"Yes, thank you."

The pilot's voice came over the loudspeaker. "Please fasten your seat belts. We'll be taking off shortly. Flying time is approximately eight hours. Mr. Hinton, there is a bed in the back of the plane for you to sleep on during the flight."

Ray looked at the flight attendant. "Where are we going?"

"We are flying to London. The Queen of England is waiting to meet you."

"Of course. Thank you." He waited until they were in the air, and then he walked to the back of the plane. There was a beautiful king-size bed with a velvet comforter and the blanket his mom had made him when he was a baby. There were dozens of soft pillows all over the bed, and when he climbed into the sheets, they smelled like freshly mowed lawns and magnolia blossoms.

The plane landed, and Ray stepped off to a waiting limousine. Buckingham Palace guards stood beside the car, and one saluted him and held open the door as he climbed in. Ray's suit was cream colored, and his tie a deep royal blue. When his car arrived at the palace, a whole regiment of guards—complete with the tall, furry black hats—stood at attention. Ray was brought through a large hallway, and two servants stood outside a grand ballroom. They bowed to Ray and opened up the double doors. He walked inside, and there she was. The Queen of England. She was wearing a blue dress that perfectly matched his tie, and a crown made of gold and rubies.

"Mr. Hinton." The Queen held out her hand, and Ray bowed deeply and kissed the back of it.

"Your Majesty."

"Please join me for tea, Mr. Hinton. It is an honor to meet you."

"The honor is all mine, and please, call me Ray."

The Queen laughed, and more servants came in with tiny sandwiches and cakes and tarts, and they served tea that smelled like milk and honey and home.

"What can I do to help you, Mr. Hinton . . . Ray?" the Queen asked. "You don't deserve to be on death row. You must let me help you."

"Being here with you is help enough," Ray answered.

"Well, you must come see me anytime you can. We must put our heads together and find a way to get you home. Everyone needs to go home."

"We'll find a way," he said. "I know I will get back home. I know it. I am praying and I am believing, and it has to happen."

"Of course you will," she said. "Now, let me show you the castle, and the gardens, and all the secret rooms we have in the palace."

Ray followed the Queen of England around for hours and hours. They played croquet and had more tea.

It felt great to be treated with respect. To be called Mr. Hinton instead of just Hinton.

"Hinton. Hinton!"

The voice came out of nowhere, and Ray could tell it startled the Queen as much as it did him. He tried to ignore it, but it only got louder, and he could see the palace guards rush in and surround the Queen as if she were under attack.

"I have to go, Your Majesty, but I will come back," he said.

"Hinton, look alive! Hinton, look alive!"

Ray blinked until his eyes seemed to focus, and then he saw the guard yelling at him. He sat up in his bed.

"You going to take your visit or what?"

He was confused. Visiting day wasn't until Friday, and it was only Wednesday.

"What are you talking about? Is my lawyer here?"

"No, you have a regular family visit. You want it or not? You've been acting strange for days."

"Of course I want it. Give me a minute to get dressed, please."

"You got exactly one minute."

Ray pulled out his dress whites. He kept one of his two sets of prison clothes just for visits, and between visits, he kept them folded and under his mattress so the creases in the pant legs would set in real sharp. He felt disoriented. If the guards wanted to give him an extra visit in the week, he wasn't going to complain.

He walked onto the visiting yard and smiled when he saw Lester, both of their moms, and Sylvia, Lester's new wife.

"How did you get an extra visit?" he asked. He was happy to see them but still confused.

"What are you going on about?" Lester laughed.

"This is our regular visit, baby. What's wrong with you?" His mom looked him up and down and furrowed her brows.

He sat down and looked at the four of them. "What day is it?" he asked.

"It's Friday. Are you sick?"

Ray looked around. The other inmates were coming out for visits too. It was morning. It was Friday. It had just been Wednesday, and now it was Friday. He had completely skipped over Thursday.

"I'm starving. Did you guys bring in some money for the vending machines?"

Lester looked at him and then stood up. He started to walk over to the vending machines but stopped a few feet away and turned back toward Ray. "Where you been, man?"

"You wouldn't believe me if I told you," Ray said. Lester shrugged and smiled at him.

Ray wasn't sure exactly what had happened. There were only two ways to leave death row. But he had just found another way. A third way. He felt better than he had in years. He jumped up to hug his mom, and even though the guards yelled at him to sit down, he held on to her. And then he started to laugh.

Time was a funny and strange and fluid thing, and now Ray knew he was going to bend it and shape it so that it wasn't his enemy. Someday he was going to walk out of there, but until then, he was going to use his mind to travel the world. He had so many places to go, and people to see, and things to learn.

"You sure you're okay?" His mom still looked worried.

"I'm sure," Ray said.

"Well, when are you coming home, baby? When are they going to let you out of here?" She always asked this question, and usually it made him sad, but not today.

"Soon, Mama," he said. "I'm going to be coming home real soon."

After his visit, the guard walked him back to his cell. Ray changed back into his regular whites and carefully folded his dress whites and put them under the mattress.

And then he sat on the edge of his bed and closed his eyes.

His mom had planted some new flowers in front of her house. They were purple and white and pink, and he ran his fingers across them gently. He walked around the side of the house. The lawn needed cutting. He opened the door of the shed and pulled the mower out. He would take care of this for her and then go inside and have some tea and let her gossip about all the goings-on at church and around town.

"Is that you, baby?" She poked her head out the screen door.

"It's me, Mama. It's me." She smiled and clapped her hands together. "I told you I would be home soon. I told you."

Chapter Thirteen

MORE THAN THE WORST THING

*"Mr. Hinton was denied effective assistance of counsel at the guilt /
innocence penalty and appellate phases of his case in violation
of his rights under the laws and Constitution of Alabama and the
Sixth, Eighth, and Fourteenth Amendments of the United States
Constitution."*

—Santha Sonenberg, 1990 petition for relief

Santha filed his petition the day before the deadline. In it,
she listed thirty-one reasons why he should be granted a
new trial—prosecutor misconduct and racial discrimination,
ineffective assistance of counsel, and not being allowed to hire
a real expert, to name just a few. Ray read the list over and over
again, and he felt hope. She had included everything, from the
polygraph test he'd passed not being allowed, to the improper
seizure of his mother's gun, to the discriminatory nature of Alabama's death penalty laws. He let some of the other guys read
it. They passed it from cell to cell.

Soon everyone was talking about his case. Ray didn't know
what some of the things on the list meant, but he used his
time in the law library to research. He had studied the amendments to the Constitution in high school but definitely needed
a refresher course. It was great just to have something new to

read, something new to talk about. Henry seemed particularly interested in his case.

"It sounds good, Ray," Henry said, "like you should be let go. You have a solid case. You really are innocent."

Ray laughed. "I know everyone says it, but I really am innocent. And I'm really going to walk out of here someday. You just wait." He didn't tell Henry that he left the row every day in his mind. He didn't tell anyone. He could be there for meals and when the guards needed him to do something, but the minute his mind wasn't occupied by the routine of the row, he left. His jet plane was always waiting, and it got easier and easier for him to travel in his mind.

Sometimes Henry would ask him what he had been doing when Henry was calling out to him, and Ray would say, "I was in Spain, Henry, but I'm back now. What do you need?"

Ray knew people thought he was losing it, but escaping in his mind gave him a sort of giddy sense of freedom. He could tune out the moaning and the roaches and the smell of death and the food that had no taste and the endless worry about who would be next to burn up in that chair. Every time an hour could pass without being aware of every slow second of that hour was a gift. Every day was like the one before it and the one after it. And there were so many days when nothing at all happened. Nothing. Just silence or moaning or guys yelling nothing at each other.

They each did their time in their own way. One guy would just draw spirals on a piece of paper—all day, every day. Spirals within spirals within spirals so that you never saw where anything ended and anything began. Some guys just spent the time between meals trying not to go crazy—they would hum, or rock themselves, or moan in a way that almost sounded like chanting. Humans were not meant to be locked in a cage, and a man couldn't survive in a box. It was cruel.

Ray knew they weren't a collection of innocent victims. Many of the guys he laughed with had done horrible things, unspeakable things. Some had committed their crimes because their minds were different and they didn't know better. Others had done things because they were high on drugs or desperate for money and never thought beyond the next moment.

The outside world called them monsters. But Ray didn't know any monsters on the row. He knew guys named Larry and Henry and Victor and Jesse. He knew Vernon and Willie and Jimmy. Not monsters. Guys with names who didn't have mothers who loved them or anyone who had ever shown them a kindness that was even close to love. Guys who were born broken or had been broken by life. Guys who had been abused as children and had their minds and their hearts warped by cruelty and violence and isolation long before they ever stood in front of a judge and a jury.

Ray was there with these guys part of the time, but the rest of the time, he left. He watched college football games in his mind, and he learned to fly a helicopter. He had a boat and a Cadillac and went on dates with lots of women. He would eat at the finest restaurants, wear the nicest clothes, and visit the most beautiful and wondrous places in the world. Traveling in his mind was like reading a good book and being transported to a completely different world, and a part of him felt a little guilty that he could escape this way when so many guys were suffering.

The State responded to his petition and basically denied

everything Santha had claimed, saying that all his claims were "procedurally barred" because an issue was either already raised during his trial or in Perhacs's direct appeal, or it could have been raised on his direct appeal but wasn't.

It didn't make any sense to Ray. It didn't seem to matter that he was innocent, that people lied, that there were real issues with his trial—the State didn't want to admit that anything was wrong, and unless you knew it was wrong or should have known it was wrong or could have known it was wrong but didn't, you couldn't argue it. Henry explained it to Ray. "If your attorney could have raised something during your trial and first appeal but didn't, it's barred by the State. If it was raised at trial or in your first appeal, and you were still convicted and denied, it's also barred by the State."

"But doesn't that cover everything?" Ray asked. "I mean everything that you would appeal on?"

"Pretty much."

It didn't seem fair or right that the odds were stacked against him—against all of them. If you couldn't afford to get an attorney at your trial or appeal, it seemed like you would never be able to prove you were innocent. A hearing was set for April 23, 1991, but then at the beginning of the month Ray got a note from Santha saying that his hearing was being postponed. She sent him a copy of the official notice she filed with the court withdrawing as his attorney. She couldn't represent him anymore because of a new job in D.C., but she said that another attorney would be taking over. Bryan Stevenson's office would send someone. She told him that they were going to amend his petition and change the hearing date and that it was now called a Rule 32 hearing because Alabama changed the rules of appellate law, but not to worry.

Not to worry.

Ray tried not to take it too hard. He called Lester and asked him to check in with the resource center in Montgomery. "Try to get hold of this Bryan Stevenson and see if he knows anything about a new attorney," he asked. "Tell him I'm innocent and that I was supposed to have a hearing on my petition." Lester always took care of things for Ray. He still drove to Holman every week, even though he had been turned away a few times because the prison was on lockdown or there weren't enough guards at work that day.

Ever since Ray had passed around his petition, guys were sharing their appeals as well. They started to have lively legal debates on their side of the row, but it was hard to yell to each other and know exactly who was talking and to who.

"Listen to this!" Ray yelled out his cell as he read aloud from the petition. "'The kind of justice a criminal defendant has cannot depend on how much money he has.'"

The guys debated this up and down the row all day.

Money determined everything, and none of them had any money.

One night a guy named Jimmy told Ray, "Hays has money. If anyone's going to get out of this place, it's Hays."

"Who's Hays?" Ray asked.

"Henry. Henry Hays. The KKK guy. You know the KKK has money. He will get out."

Henry Hays?

Ray couldn't believe it. He knew who Henry Hays was.

Everybody in Alabama knew that he and a couple of other white guys had lynched a Black boy named Michael Donald in Mobile in 1981. (It was the Ku Klux Klan's last "official" lynching; the civil suit that Donald's mother later won against them effectively bankrupted the organization.) The kid had been a teenager, nineteen years old, and the KKK was mad that a Black guy on trial might get away with killing a white policeman. Ray thought it had been a mistrial, but he couldn't remember. Henry Hays's father was rumored to be the head of the KKK or something. That poor Donald boy had been randomly picked up and beaten and brutally murdered. His mother had sued the Klan or taken some other legal action. He couldn't remember exactly, but he remembered being sickened by the murder. Michael Donald hadn't been much younger than Ray was—five or six years—and the story had reminded him of the bombs growing up and the kids who had the dogs let loose on them and the girls who had been murdered in the church. The news about the lynching had angered him.

All this time, Ray had had no idea that his friend Henry was actually *Henry Hays*.

Ray went back to his cell that night and stared at the ceiling. He was Henry's friend. Henry knew Ray was Black. Ray wanted to talk to him. He wanted to understand.

"Henry!" he yelled.

"What you want, Ray?"

"I just figured out who you are. I didn't know." There was no answer right away, and Ray wondered what Henry was thinking.

"Everything my mom and dad taught me was a lie, Ray. Everything they taught me against Blacks, it was a lie."

Ray didn't know exactly what to say back to him. "You know,

just about everything I believe about people, I learned from my mom."

"So you know what I mean," he said.

"Yeah. I do. I guess I was just lucky that my mom taught me to love people, no matter what. She taught me to forgive."

"You was lucky, Ray. You was really lucky."

"She taught me to have compassion for everybody, Henry, and I have compassion for you. I'm sorry your mama and your daddy didn't teach you the same. I really am."

"Me too."

They didn't say much after that, but the row was pretty quiet that night. Sometimes you need to make family where you find it, and Ray knew that to survive he had to make a family of these men and they had to make a family of him. It didn't matter who was Black and who was white—all that kind of fell away when you lived a few feet away from an electric chair. They all faced execution. They all were scrambling to survive.

Not monsters.

Not the worst thing they had ever done.

They were so much more than what they had been reduced to—so much more than could be contained in one small cage.

On the next visiting day, Henry had a visit too. Ray sat with Lester and Sylvia, and they were laughing about something when Ray heard Henry call his name.

"Ray! Ray, come here for a second." He gestured Ray over. Henry sat with an older couple; Ray assumed they were his parents.

Ray glanced toward the guard, but he wasn't paying him any mind, so Ray walked over to Henry's table.

"Ray, I want you to meet my father, Bennie. Dad, this is Ray Hinton. My friend."

Ray held out his hand to Henry's father. He just looked at him and then down at the table. He didn't say hello, and he wouldn't shake Ray's hand.

"He's my friend. My best friend." Henry's voice shook a little bit.

His mom smiled at Ray faintly, and then the guard yelled to Ray to go sit down.

"Nice to meet you both," Ray said, and he walked back to his table.

"What was that all about?" asked Lester.

"That was about some progress, my friend, some crazy progress on death row."

Ray imagined it took a lot for Henry to stand up to his dad. To tell him that this large Black man was his best friend. They never talked about the fact that Henry's father wouldn't shake his hand. They just kept on living next to each other and surviving as best they could.

Ray's new attorney came to see him a few months later. His name was Alan Black. He was from Boston.

Ray had always been a Yankees fan.

"I'm going to ask Bryan Stevenson for some money to hire someone to test the bullets again. We need a new expert. We need to prove there's no way your mother's gun was used to kill those men."

Ray nodded. He had thought about this before. Payne had been destroyed on the stand, and even though he had told the truth, no one believed him. No one would ever believe him when he couldn't even operate the machinery or find the light on the microscope.

"I need you to get the best of the best," Ray said.

Alan Black nodded and kind of laughed nervously. He didn't look Ray in the eye, so while he wasn't who Ray would pick as his attorney, Ray was grateful he was there.

"I'll see what I can do," he said. "I think I know a guy out of Jersey. I'll talk to Bryan."

"Okay, you do that. It might be good if you find someone from the South, though. Judges around here don't really like guys from out of town." Ray didn't want to tell him what to do; that hadn't worked out so well with Perhacs.

Ray went back to his cell after the visit, and Henry asked how it went.

"Well, Henry, it's like this. I can get over the fact that you used to be in the KKK, but I'm not sure I'm going to be able to get over the fact that my life is now in the hands of a Red Sox fan."

Henry and some of the other guys started laughing.

Ray smiled. As long as he was making them laugh, they were all still alive.

He was tired of talking through the bars, though. He was tired of standing with his mouth pressed against dirty mesh wire every time he wanted to talk to another human.

Ray thought about Wallace and his Project Hope. He thought about passing his list of thirty-one reasons up and down the row.

"Henry!" he yelled.

"Yeah?"

"I'm thinking about starting a book club."

"A what?"

"A book club. I'm going to see if we can meet in the library once a month and have ourselves a book club. You in?"

Henry paused a moment. "I'm in," he said.

"I want in!" yelled a guy named Larry.

"Me too!"

"Who's that?" Ray asked.

"It's Victor. I want in. What are we going to read, though? Wouldn't your book club just be a Bible study?"

"No, I'm going to get some real books in here. I'm going to talk to the warden, and we're going to get some real books," Ray said. "And we're going to have ourselves a little club."

He closed his eyes. He could leave the row in his mind, and now he was going to show these guys that they could leave too. Ray could remember being in school and reading a book about California and getting so lost in it, he swore he could smell the salt water of the Pacific Ocean.

He just needed to get some books.

Then they could all leave that place together.

Chapter Fourteen

CATCHING FLIES
WITH HONEY

"It's important to understand how someone who has money is able to buy their way out of jail or prison, so you're much better off in our justice system if you're rich and guilty than if you're poor and innocent."

—Sam Brooke, Deputy Director of the
Southern Poverty Law Center (SPLC)[22]

The first thing Alan Black did was ask Judge Garrett for money for experts to investigate Ray's case. Judge Garrett granted the motions, and Ray wondered why he would give money now in the appeal when he wouldn't give the money in Ray's actual trial. If Ray had had money, Perhacs could have found someone better than Payne. If he'd had money, they could have had an expert prove Ray couldn't have driven from work to Quincy's that fast. If he'd had money, he could have gotten an attorney who felt like he was paid for his time.

If he'd had money, he probably wouldn't have been arrested in the first place.

It always seemed to come down to the money.

Ray received a copy of all his legal filings in the mail, and it

---

22 www.davisvanguard.org/2019/03/court-fines-and-fees-are-literally-trapping
-poor-people-in-the-system-for-life/

was the only mail the guards couldn't open or mess with. Any letter you wrote had to remain unsealed so the prison staff could read it before it was mailed. Any letter that came in was also read by the prison staff. Every phone call was recorded. Ray couldn't understand why they had to read the letters that went out, but it became clear that they didn't want inmates to complain about how they were being treated. They didn't want someone to call in the attorneys. Holman was always short staffed, and the row was no different. The prisoners were like lab rats being closely monitored for any potential signs of revolt. Ray knew it was easier for them to keep the men in their cages where they couldn't get into trouble rather than let them out. Summers were the worst. They didn't allow any fans in the cells because they could be broken apart to use as weapons, but with the tight wire mesh covering the doors, there was zero ventilation or flow of air. It was over 100 degrees outside during the summer months, and in the cells, it had to be 110 or 120. It was like being in a sauna, and some days it felt like you were actually slow roasting. It's hard to talk, much less fight, when it is so hot you can barely move or take a breath. Much like the staff reading their mail and recording their conversations, the heat was a way to keep control, but the heat also made some guys erratic and even more violent. Ray knew that all the warden wanted was to keep the peace, especially on death row, where it was assumed that they had nothing to lose and would kill if given the chance. But he also knew the warden was going about it all wrong, and it was having the opposite effect.

"Hinton, lunch!" The officer who yelled looked just as hot as Ray was.

"Hey, I need to ask you something," Ray said.

"What's that, Hinton?" He sounded annoyed and tired.

"I need to borrow your truck."

"What?"

"I need to borrow your truck. Just for a little bit. I'll bring it back with a full tank of gas, don't you worry about that."

"What the hell are you talking about?"

"I know this cool little swimming hole. It's hidden back in some trees outside of Jefferson County. There's an old, unmarked dirt road that leads to it, so not a lot of people know about it. You have to walk a bit through the woods. It's shady, and the water is so clear you can see right to the bottom. I think it's fed by an underground spring or something. The water is so clear and so cool you can drink it. I'm going to need to borrow your truck, and I'll bring it back later tonight, I promise. I just need to have myself a float in that spring water. Cool myself down, you know?"

The guard just stared at Ray, like Ray had finally lost it.

"Maybe we should go together? Get out of here and cool off? Otherwise, I just need your keys and you can keep working, and I'll be back before shift change. I heard you talking about your new truck, and I promise I'll take good care of it."

The guard started laughing and shaking his head. "I don't think so, Hinton, but here's your lunch."

And just like that, the guard was smiling at Ray.

"I need to talk to the warden about something," Ray said, smiling back at him. "Can you get him a message or let the captain know?"

"I'll bring you some paper, and you write it down and I'll get it to him."

"Thanks."

The guard shook his head at Ray, but he was still smiling as he moved on down the row delivering lunch.

"You making friends with the guards, Ray?" Ray could hear the scorn in Walter Hill's voice. Hill had killed another inmate at another prison before Holman and was now on the row for a triple murder, so he was one of the guys who the warden thought had nothing to lose. He was angry all the time. Ray couldn't blame him for that. Ray also wasn't going to judge him. He didn't know Walter Hill's story. Whatever he had done was between him and God.

"Hey, Walter!" Ray yelled. "You know what my sweet mama always says to me?"

Walter didn't answer the question. "They're not your friends, Ray. They trying to kill us, and I don't like nobody who gets cozy with the guards. You know what I'm saying?"

Ray knew what he was saying. Outside of death row, any inmate who seemed like they were friendly to the guards was considered a snitch. Snitches didn't do well in Holman. At all. You could get your throat cut if anyone suggested you were a snitch. Ray didn't know who Walter had killed in general population or why, but it didn't matter, and Ray wasn't going to let him or anyone intimidate him.

Ray raised his voice so they would hear him on the other side of the row. "My mama always told me that you get more flies with honey than with vinegar."

"I heard that before," said Victor.

"Just because you pour out some honey doesn't mean you're a fly. You hear me, Walter? It's how you catch the flies. It's how we got an extra fifteen minutes on the yard. You use the vinegar. I'm going to use the honey."

Ray left it at that. He knew the guards were doing a job. Just like Ray hadn't dreamed of going into the coal mines and had hated every minute of it, he imagined most of them hadn't grown up dreaming of someday working on death row. They were all getting through this life the best they could, and it was up to them to figure out what happened next. It was hell on the row—every minute of every day—but in this hell, it could always get worse. Ray thought that maybe it could also get a little better. He was going to do his part to make it that way. His mama had taught him about getting flies with honey, and she had also taught him that you had to work within the system. You couldn't grow up Black in the South and not know how to work within the system. It was the same at Holman—some people held all the power, and there were all kinds of ways you could fight back. He didn't believe violence was ever a way to get what he wanted. It didn't work in the real world, and it definitely didn't work on the row.

If Ray wanted the guards to cooperate, he had to cooperate. It was a trade-off. He knew others, like Hill, would take his cooperation the wrong way, but it was about survival. Not just for himself but for all of them on the row. Ray had people who loved him and came to visit every week. Lester made sure there was money in his prison account so he could buy essentials. He had grown up with unconditional love. He had faith and a God and a Bible that promised him he would get out of there someday. Ray was better off than a lot of the guys next to him. They were all facing death, but he was facing it with love all around him. He tried to focus on that more than the fact that his life had been stolen from him. Ray didn't know who else was innocent. Maybe every other guy sitting in his rat cage was innocent too.

Who knew? Maybe every other guy in his rat cage had killed. It didn't matter. They were slowly roasting to death, and making it worse for themselves was not a way to get payback. It only hurt them more. Ray decided he was going to do what he could with what he had. A little bit of kindness was amplified on death row, because it was so unexpected. *You can scream out in a crowd of voices also screaming out, and no one hears you—but when you yell into the silence, your voice sounds louder.* Ray was going to be that kind voice screaming out on the row, and he was going to make it better for everyone. They were all the same there, all discarded like garbage and deemed unworthy to have a life.

Ray was going to prove them wrong.

Charlie Jones looked every bit like the stereotype of a Southern redneck warden, straight down to his cowboy boots with spurs and a face that was white and fleshy and soft. He had a tough job—keeping a handle on things at the most violent prison in the country. Every day, he was responsible for his staff and an inmate population that would riot if given the chance. Ray was very aware of all this going into his conversation with Jones.

"I hear you're a talker, Hinton. And I hear that the guys listen to you. I still don't know why you didn't want to talk on camera when Geraldo was here."

Geraldo Rivera had spent a night on death row, brought in cameras, and pretended to be one of the prisoners. Worn whites and slept overnight in a cell, but it was all a joke. A stunt, a pretend game where he was able to leave the next day. Rivera didn't and couldn't know what it was like to be locked in a cage when you were innocent. He was playing a game that he knew nothing about, and it was clear to Ray that he only did it for his own ego. The guys on the row saw the show. Geraldo made sure he had his shirt off. Usually, the meals were made in the main jail and sat out in the open, uncovered, as they traveled through the prison before they got to inmates on death row. When they handed Geraldo his tray of food they had another tray over it to keep out the dirt and the dust and rat hairs and the cockroach pieces. The actual inmates didn't get their food served to them with a cover on it—and that small difference said it all.

"Well, I would have if you had sent me to New York to film the show. Why, I could have flown on an airplane for the first time and had some of those little peanuts I hear are so good. I was ready to be on the show if it meant I could have some of those peanuts."

The warden laughed. "Now, what's this I hear about a club of some kind?"

"I want to start a book club. I was thinking we could meet once a month in the library. But we need to be able to read something other than the Bible. Not everyone cares for the Bible like we do. You know what I mean?"

"Yeah, and it's a damn shame," he said.

"So my best friend, Lester, said he would mail a few books here, and we could read them and then have ourselves a discussion."

The warden looked down, and Ray could see he was considering his proposal.

"Look," Ray said. "These guys need something to focus on besides what the guards are doing and not doing for them. Besides the heat. Besides the fact that our food tastes like dirt. You know? It's a way to keep the peace. A book club will help things stay more peaceful."

The warden nodded.

"You can't have guys spending twenty-three hours a day thinking about death. It makes them crazy. And when people go crazy, who knows what they'll do." It may have been a bit much, but it was the truth. Ray wanted him to believe that if they had books on the row, it would keep the inmates quiet. But really, he knew that it would set them free. If the guys had books, they could travel the world. They would get smarter and freer. There was a reason back in the days of slavery the plantation owners didn't want the enslaved people to learn to read. Charlie Jones might have had family who once owned Ray's family, but Ray wasn't going to bring that up. He wasn't going to show him anything but how a book club would keep the peace.

"Let me think on it, Hinton. You make a good point, but let me talk to my officers. They're the ones who are there. I don't want any trouble from death row. You understand what I'm saying? I let you have some extra time out on the yard, and that's been all right. But if I have any trouble from the row, we'll just keep you guys in for the full twenty-four, you understand? Take away them visits if anything gets to be a problem. I got a lot of guys in here who need to be managed."

"Yes, sir," Ray said. "I appreciate you taking the time to consider it. I do think it will help your men have an easier time doing their jobs, sir. Thank you for considering my proposal."

Ray's manners seemed to puzzle Charlie Jones. He tilted his head like he couldn't quite figure out if Ray was joking or serious.

"They listen to you, Hinton. You keep things peaceful on the row, and I'll see what I can do. I can't have a bunch of you in the library at once. I don't have the staff for that. Four guys, maybe six. I'll think about it."

"Thank you."

"And we don't have a budget to be buying books. You'd have to have them mailed to us, and we'd inspect them first. No more than two books at a time. I can't see what it would hurt to let some other books on the row."

"That's a good idea, sir."

"Anything else, Hinton? I think we understand each other here. Anything else going on I need to know about?" And there it was: Just like that, he wanted Ray to be an informer, but Ray wasn't playing that game.

"Well, about Geraldo, sir. Some of the guys noticed he got a tray turned upside down on top of his food tray to keep the dirt out. You know, as a lid on his food. And some of the guys thought this was a great idea. Was that your idea when Geraldo was here?" Ray paused then, and Jones nodded and smiled. "It was a great idea. I think it would go a long way if we could use that great idea for all of us, get lids on our food to keep the dust out. You know how dusty it is in here."

"All right, then, I don't see why not. I'll let the kitchen know."

"Thank you, sir."

Ray smiled all the way back to his cell. And when the captain of the guard let him know that book club was approved for six guys, he told Lester on visiting day.

"Can you send in a couple of books to the prison? Send them to the attention of the warden."

"What you up to now?" asked Lester.

"I'm starting a book club."

"A what?"

"You know, a book club. We're going to read books and then meet once a month as a club to talk about them."

Lester's new wife, Sylvia, had come with him to visit. Her nickname was Sia.

"What you laughing at, Sia?" Ray asked. "You never heard of a book club before?"

"I've heard of it, but I think it's funny that you guys are going to sit around having a book club. What books are you going to read?"

"I'm not sure. What do you think?"

Lester kind of shrugged. He wasn't a big reader, but Sia looked serious all of a sudden.

"I know," she said. "You guys need to read James Baldwin, Harper Lee, Maya Angelou. I just read *I Know Why the Caged Bird Sings*; you guys need to read that one. And *To Kill a Mockingbird* and *Go Tell It on the Mountain*." Sia was getting excited about the idea.

"Okay," Ray said, "you send us the books. I'll pay you guys back when I get out of here, I promise. Just send me two books, care of Charlie Jones. We'll have to read and pass them around to share. You send them in whatever order you think we should read them first. Maybe we could talk about them when you visit, and you could help me think of how to talk about them in book club. How about that?"

Sia nodded. "Let's start with James Baldwin."

"James Baldwin it is. He's going to take these guys right out of death row!"

"What do you mean?" Lester looked at Ray, puzzled.

"Not everyone has my imagination. All day, every day, guys are drowning in fear and death. Imagine knowing the day you're going to die. How could you think about anything else? These guys have to find a way to think about life."

At that moment, there was yelling across the yard. Guards rushed over to another visiting table. Ray saw Henry jump up and then get pulled back by a guard. Sirens went off, and that meant they had to lie facedown on the ground.

"Don't worry. It's okay," Ray said to Lester and Sia, who looked scared. Ray was glad his mom hadn't felt well enough to make the drive. This would have frightened her too. He turned his head and looked over to Henry. He had been having a visit too, but Ray could see his dad was on the ground and the guards were around him. Ray wondered what had happened. He met Henry's eyes, and Henry looked afraid.

"Visit's over! All inmates return to cells."

Ray could hear ambulance sirens in the distance. He turned back to wave goodbye to Lester and Sia, but they were being taken out and didn't see him. Henry lined up behind Ray for count.

"What happened?" Ray asked.

"My dad was going off about my trial that's coming up, and then he just fell over. I think it's his heart. He turned completely white, almost blue."

Ray could hear Henry's voice shake. Henry's father was a racist, murdering man—but he was still his dad.

"I'm sorry, man. I really am. I hope he's okay."

"You know they declared a mistrial, because of his heart, before."

"Yeah," Ray said. The trial of Bennie Hays had been in the papers, and everyone knew about it, even though Henry never talked about it.

"I'm sorry, Henry. I really am."

"Thanks, Ray. Thanks for everything."

Henry hung his head and didn't talk anymore. The next day, Saturday, Henry's father died. The guard came to give Henry the news.

Ray prayed for Bennie Hays. He prayed that in death he would know more than he did in life. Someone had taught Bennie Hays to hate, and Bennie Hays had taught his son Henry to hate. And now Henry was learning that hate didn't get him anywhere.

In Alabama, when someone dies, you bring food to the family. All day long, friends and neighbors show up with casseroles, pies, or some homemade grits. It's the way to show love and support. By the end of the first day of grieving, the family's fridge and table and counters are covered with food. Food is love and life and comfort and one small way to show others you are there wanting to nourish and nurture them in their grief.

As soon as the guard left Henry's cell, Ray passed some coffee out of his cell to Henry. The guys next to Ray reached out and took it from Ray and passed it down to the guy next to him. Up and down the row, all day long, men who might just as soon kill each other as look at each other on the streets passed their precious food items to Henry's cell—candy bars and soup and coffee and small pieces of chocolate and even fruit. Anyone who had something of value ordered from commissary or left over from a meal passed it one to the other until it reached Henry. Nobody took it for himself. Nobody interrupted the chain of comfort as it wound its way up and down and around the row until it reached Henry.

They all knew grief. They all knew sorrow.

They all knew what it was like to be alone.

And they all were beginning to learn that you can make a family out of anyone.

Even the guards, perhaps caught up in their own humanity or because Henry's dad had collapsed under their watch, helped pass the food to Henry.

In a twisted way, they were also a part of this big, strange family on death row. They were the ones charged with the prisoners' care every day—obligated to help them when they were sick yet also the ones who walked them to their deaths, strapped them into the chair, and then turned their backs as the warden flipped the switch to end their lives.

In the end, Ray thought, they were all just trying to find their way.

Chapter Fifteen

A READER LIVES A THOUSAND LIVES

"Stories have given me a place in which to lose myself. They have allowed me to remember. They have allowed me to forget. They have allowed me to imagine different endings and better possible worlds."

—Roxane Gay

The books were a big deal. Nobody had books on death row. They had never been allowed, and it was like someone had brought in contraband. Only six guys were allowed to join Ray in book club (too many inmates together like that made prison officials nervous), but every guy on the row was now allowed to have two books besides the Bible in his cell. Some didn't care, but others made calls out to family and friends to let them know they could send in a book or two. It had to be a brand-new book and be sent directly from a bookstore to the prison, that was how they tried to keep contraband from being smuggled in inside books. It was like a whole new world opened up, and guys started talking about what books they liked. Some guys didn't know how to read, others had learning difficulties and had never been to school beyond a few grades. Those guys didn't know why they were on death row, and Ray wondered about a world that would just as soon execute a guy as treat him in a hospital or admit he wasn't mentally capable of knowing right from wrong.

The very first book club meeting consisted of Jesse Morrison, Victor Kennedy, Larry Heath, Brian Baldwin, Ed Horsley, Henry, and Ray. They were allowed to meet in the law library, but they each had to sit at a different table. They couldn't get up. In order to talk to everyone at once, you had to kind of swivel around in your seat so no one felt left out. If someone wanted to read something out of the book, they had to toss the book to each other and hope that the guy caught it or it landed in reach of someone because they weren't allowed to lift their butts up off the seats. The guards seemed nervous when they walked the men to the library. They weren't planning a riot or an escape; they were five Black guys and two white guys talking about a James Baldwin book. *Perfectly normal. Nothing to see here.*

When the books arrived, one of the guards had brought them to Ray's cell and handed them to him. Two brand-new copies of James Baldwin's *Go Tell It on the Mountain*. Ray had read it in high school, but he read it again so he could pass it on to the next guy. All seven of the book club members took about a week to read the book, so with two copies being passed, they were ready for book club in a month. That became the routine for each book. Some other guys had asked their families to send them the same book, so in Ray's section of the row—with fourteen guys upstairs and fourteen guys downstairs—almost everybody seemed to be talking about the book.

Some people hated it because it talked so much about God, and others loved it for the same reason.

A couple liked it because there were some sex scenes.

For that month, it seemed like the row was transformed to another place. They were in New York City, in Harlem. Their parents had a complicated and sordid past, and no relationship was as it seemed to be on the surface. They were in church, waiting to be saved or feeling the glory of Jesus as it racked their bodies in convulsions.

They were victims of violence.

They were caught up in a strange family dynamic where they didn't know who their daddy was or why they hated him. They were each John, the main character, turning fourteen and trying to figure out the world and make sense of what he was feeling. They were themselves, but at the same time they were different, and the book occupied their days and nights in a new way.

They weren't discussing legal questions, playing pretend lawyers and trying to understand a system that didn't make sense half the time. They weren't the scum of the earth, the lowest of the low, the forgotten and abandoned men who were sitting in a dark corner of hell waiting for their turn to walk to the electric chair. They were transported, and just as Ray could travel the world and have tea with the Queen of England, he watched these men be transported in their minds for a small chunk of time. It was a vacation from the row—and everyone was a part of book club, even before the seven official members had their first official meeting.

When they finally did have their meeting, they sat at their respective tables and felt an awkwardness that wasn't there when they were yelling to each other through the cell bars. Larry and Henry, the only white guys, looked especially uncomfortable. The guards had locked them into the library, so they were in there by themselves. There could be no violating the rules, no getting in any fights, no foolishness whatsoever. It was strange after so many years to have a change in routine. Every day, except for when they took you to shower, things happened at the same exact time. So when there was suddenly something new, especially for the guys like Baldwin and Heath and Horsley, who had been there over a decade, it was strange and they seemed on edge.

"So, what do you think?" Ray asked everyone.

"How do we do this, exactly? What's the format?" Jesse Morrison was used to Project Hope, so he knew how to organize a group.

Everyone looked at Ray. "Let's just talk about whatever we read that we want to talk about. Whether we liked the book or not. What we liked about it, what we didn't. What left an impression. How does that sound?" He looked around at everyone, and they nodded. Henry looked serious. "You know what I liked?" Ray asked. "I liked this sentence: 'For the rebirth of the soul was perpetual; only rebirth every hour could stay the hand of Satan.'"

"What you like about it?" asked Larry.

"I like that it's about hope," Ray said. "It's like your soul can be reborn. No matter what you've done, you can be new again. It's a hopeful sentence."

"Yeah, but Satan is right there, pushing you every hour on the hour," said Victor. Victor was a quiet guy. "When I drink, Satan takes over; that much I know."

The men were quiet. Everyone knew Victor had been drunk the night he had committed the horrible crime that had gotten him a death sentence.

Heath spoke like a preacher, so Ray expected him to have something to say about the church folk in Baldwin's book. He was strangely quiet, though.

"Everybody talking about being saved in this book," said Henry. "I've never been to a church where people are falling on the ground getting saved."

Ray laughed. "Well, you never been to a Black church, Henry. When we get out of here, I'm going to take you to a church where you will see the Holy Spirit come down and take over a person's body so much that it looks like that person is going to fly right up and out the window of that church!" He started laughing. "You are not going to believe how people carry on in a Black church. The only problem is it's going to last all day and into the night, so you'd best be prepared to eat before you go and be ready to sit there until the Spirit moves you. You are going to be singing and praising the Lord like you've never praised the Lord before!"

Henry looked around the group. "I'm not sure they're going to want me in there—you know, not everyone is like you guys."

"Well, we will have to show them, won't we? We will have to show them how a man can change."

Henry smiled at Ray and kind of shook his head and shrugged a little. They all knew the row was different. Outside of the prison, the world was still different. Ray looked around at his unlikely group, locked in a library in Holman Prison. A few of them were innocent, a few were not. It didn't really matter.

"This is what I liked," said Baldwin. "The part where John's having to clean the house. Do you remember? Right in the beginning?" Baldwin unfolded a piece of paper he had brought with him. "I wrote it down while I was reading." He straightened out the paper and cleared his throat before he began reading, softly and carefully, like he had been practicing and didn't want to get it wrong.

Everyone was quiet when Baldwin finished.

"Are you like the guy pushing the boulder up the hill?" asked Victor after a while.

"Yeah, pretty much." Baldwin cleared his throat. "Aren't we all pushing the boulder? Every day, all day, week after week, year after year, we push that boulder up, and then the giant just pushes it back down. And we're going to keep doing this until the giant crushes us to death with that boulder, or someone comes along at the top of the hill and gives us a hand. Someone tells the giant to make way, and we get to push our boulder up and over and then sit down and take a rest or something? Isn't that just how it is?"

A few guys laughed, but Ray nodded at Baldwin. Horsley just looked down. Ray had been pushing his boulder up the hill hoping that Perhacs, or Santha, or now Alan Black was going to move the giant out of the way. Or at least hold him back so Ray could get to the top. He knew what Baldwin meant. He knew how helpless he felt. Ray felt the same way.

"That's a good quote, Brian," Ray said. "That's something we can all relate to."

The others nodded.

Horsley raised his hand to speak, and they all laughed. "What you want to say, Ed?" Ray asked.

"I like how you think the people are all a certain way, but then you find out their stories, their histories, and you see how they got to be that way." He went on, "It seems like the more you know of their story, the more you kind of forgive them for what they do. You know? It's kind of like that here, right? We all got a story that led to another story and led to some choices and big mistakes. All these characters make mistakes, you know? Nobody is living this life perfect." Larry hung his head, but the other guys grunted in agreement.

Then it was quiet, and Ray wondered who was thinking about their own mistakes. Ray had made mistakes, no doubt about it. Wouldn't anyone do things over if they could, when they knew better? There wasn't a guy in this library who wouldn't have chosen differently if he could have, Ray knew that for sure.

"Who else read a passage that meant something to them?" Ray asked. He wasn't sure if this was how a book club was held in other places, but he didn't have a study guide or a printed list of questions from anywhere.

Ray had talked to Sia and Lester about it on their last visit, and Sia had said to just let people talk about what moved them. "Everybody feels something different when they read the same thing. You just have to see what made people feel something and then talk about that," she'd said. "Don't try to be the teacher; just talk about whatever the guys want to talk about."

Ray had nodded. The point was to get them thinking about anything but the dark, grimy, hot hell of the row. It was a gift to spend time in your mind away from your own reality. Ray could take his private jet anywhere around the world. He spent his week between visits having dinner with the most beautiful women in the world. He had already won Wimbledon five times. He was just this week being recruited by the New York Yankees. Ray was busy in his cell, too busy to think about the giant at the top of the hill pushing his boulder down. That's all he wanted for these guys, an hour of freedom and escape. An hour away from the rats and the roaches and the smell of death and decay. He felt like they were all slowly dying from their own fear— their minds killing them quicker than the State of Alabama ever could.

Bring in the books, he thought. *Let every man on the row have a week away, inside the world of a book.* Ray knew if the mind could open, the heart would follow. He'd seen it happen to Henry. Henry, now sitting there in a locked room with five Black men who had nothing to lose. Henry had been taught to hate and fear Black people so much that he had thought it was in his rights to go find a teenage boy and beat and stab and lynch him just because of the color of his skin. Ray had no anger toward Henry, because he understood that Henry had spent his life learning to fear Black people. He had been trained to hate. It sounded bizarre, but: Death row had been good for Henry. Death row had saved his soul. Death row had taught him that his hate was wrong.

"What about you, Ray?" someone asked.

Ray looked around at the guys. "You know how he's walking in the city, I think on Fifth Avenue, and he knows it's not the place for him?"

"Where's that part at?" asked Victor.

"I don't remember exactly, but he's being taught that the whites don't like him, but he remembers a white teacher being nice to him when he's sick. He thinks someday that the white people will honor him. Respect him. Do you guys remember that?" Ray said.

Henry cleared his throat. "I remember that part because it was like the opposite of what I was taught, but just the same, you know?" He looked around a bit nervously. "I wrote it down too." Henry took out his own paper—a piece of inmate stationery with the lines printed on it as if the inmates were too dumb to write straight. "Can I read it?" he asked.

Everybody nodded. "It reminded me of my dad. I thought of him, so I wrote it down."

"You go ahead and read it," Ray said. "Let's hear it."

Henry began: "'This was not my father's opinion. My father said that all white people were wicked, and that God was going to bring them low. He said that white people were never to be trusted, and that they told nothing but lies,'" Henry read. He went on reading aloud about all the ways white people had tried to destroy Black people, how the world told Black people that "'For him there was the back door, and the dark stairs, and the kitchen or the basement. This world was not for him. If he refused to believe, and wanted to break his neck trying, then he could try until the sun refused to shine; they would never let him enter. In John's mind then, the people and the avenue underwent a change, and he feared them and he knew that one day he could hate them if God did not change his heart.'"

The book club was quiet when Henry finished. They all knew why Henry had picked that passage. His family was KKK. And here was this kid's dad teaching him the same exact thing, only opposite.

"It's a shame," said Henry. "What fathers teach sons. It's a sin to hate, ain't that right, preacher man?" Henry looked over at Heath.

"That's right. It's a sin to hate, but God can forgive our sins. And the sins of our fathers."

"That was a good passage, Henry," said Victor, and both Horsley and Baldwin nodded. Five Black men in the South were trying to comfort the white man who would forever be known for doing the last lynching of a Black boy.

"I don't believe the world is not for him," Ray said. "Or for anyone. We are all God's children, and this world belongs to all of us. I know the sun will never refuse to shine. We may not see it, but I know it's there. I'm not going to have hate in my heart. I spent some dark years here with nothing but hate in my heart. I can't live like that."

"You are not a hater, Ray," said Jesse.

"My mama didn't raise me to hate. And I'm sorry for anyone who was taught to hate instead of love, to fight instead of help. I'm sorry for that and for anyone in this room who feels shame for what they were taught." He looked at Henry. "God knows what's in each man's heart. What someone did or didn't do is between a man and God and is none of anyone else's business."

Everyone nodded, and Ray could see the guard walking up to unlock the door. Book club had been a success. They had spent an hour talking about something that mattered.

"Someday, when I get out of here, you know what I'm going to do?" Ray asked.

"What you going to do, Ray?"

"I'm going to tell the world about how there was men in here that mattered. That cared about each other and the world. That were learning how to look at things differently."

"You're going to tell it on the mountain, Ray?" Jesse asked. The other guys laughed.

"I'm going to tell it on every single mountain there is. I'm going to push that boulder right on up and over that giant, and I'm going to stand at the top of that hill, and on the top of every mountain I can find, and I'm going to tell it. I'm going to tell his story, and I'm going to tell your story. Hell, maybe I will even write a book and tell it like that."

"Everybody up. Back in the cell. This here is over right now." Two guards rounded up the men and walked them back over to our cells. Ray watched as Henry grabbed his paper where he had carefully copied down a whole page of James Baldwin's writing and folded it back up. Who would have thought those words would have mattered so much to him?

Larry Heath was the first member of book club to die. He didn't have a last meal for dinner, and when Charlie Jones asked him for any final words, he said, "If this is what it takes for there to be healing in their lives, so be it. Father, I ask for forgiveness for my sins."

On March 20, 1992, at a little after midnight, the guards put a black bag over his head, and the warden who had allowed him the privilege of reading a book and meeting with six other guys to talk about it . . . electrocuted him until he was dead.

At the next book club, they left his chair empty.

THE BOOK CLUB BOOKLIST

- *Go Tell It on the Mountain*, James Baldwin

- *Your Blues Ain't Like Mine*, Bebe Moore Campbell

- *I Know Why the Caged Bird Sings*, Maya Angelou

- *To Kill a Mockingbird*, Harper Lee

- *Uncle Tom's Cabin*, Harriet Beecher Stowe

Chapter Sixteen

TEN THOUSAND WAYS TO LIVE IN A CAGE

"We can start to ask those in our lives that do not experience justice to tell us their story. And perhaps that story might bring some critical action steps towards engaging in the ongoing US struggle 'for liberty and justice for all.'"

—Lia Howard, *Listening to the Disenfranchised*

Ray married Halle Berry on a Sunday, one of his best day-dreams yet. They promised to love each other in sickness and in health, for better or for worse, for richer or for poorer, until death do us part, and his heart felt like it was going to burst open with happiness and joy.

"Oh, Ray," she murmured, "I love you so much. I don't know what I would have done if I hadn't met you."

Ray pledged to love and care for Halle forever. The preacher pronounced them man and wife, and Lester and his mama threw wedding rice at the couple as they ran to a white stretch limousine.

"Goodbye, everyone," Ray said. "We are traveling around the world, but we will be back in a year to see you all again."

"Goodbye, baby," his mama said as she wrapped her arms

around him and squeezed him tight. "You bring me home a grandchild, you hear me? I want twin grandbabies. A boy and a girl."

"I'll see what I can do," he said, laughing and kissing her on the cheek.

Lester shook his hand and then patted him on the back. "You did it," he said. "You found the perfect woman for you. You are a lucky man, and Halle is a lucky woman."

In his dream, Ray knew Lester was genuinely happy for him. Life was good. He embraced his new wife, Halle Berry, and—-

"Hinton! Get your butt up, Hinton! Now!"

The door slammed open, and four guards rushed into his cell and grabbed his arms. Ray felt himself pushed up against the wall, his head turned to the right so that his cheekbone pushed into the cold cement. One guard's hand was on his upper back, and they were outfitted in full riot gear with vests and weapons.

He didn't recognize these four guards. They started turning over his books and throwing his shorts and socks into the hallway outside his cell. Up went his mattress, and his perfect pressed whites that he had been working on creasing for the last few days were thrown to the ground and stepped on by a black boot. He watched as the pictures of his mama and of his nieces were thrown out into the hall as well.

"You don't like this, do you?" one of the guards asked. Ray didn't answer.

"You got a television in here and everything. Seems like death row is pretty cushy here at Holman."

Were they going to break his TV, or throw it out in the hall? They just looked under it and checked to see that there was nothing hidden behind the cord or that none of the electronics were loose.

"You got too many clothes in here. We're going to take half of them. You're not allowed to have so many shorts and socks. This isn't summer camp."

Ray watched them throw more clothes out into the hall. "You don't like this, do you?" the guard asked again.

"No, I don't," Ray answered.

"We might come back in five minutes and do this all again. We are here in your prison for twelve hours today, and your staff is over at Donaldson going through our prison. Fresh eyes see new things. Hell, we might do this every hour on the hour today, and what you gonna do about that?"

Ray could feel the man's elbow against his back, pressing him harder into the wall.

"Why don't you just move in here if you want to do that?" Ray said. "You can throw stuff around all day, then. I'll go out, and you just stay here and do what you need to do." He said it quietly, almost politely, and the three guards going through his stuff stopped for a second and turned to look at him.

One of them laughed. The other two shook their heads, and the one who had Ray up against the wall pressed in even harder.

"Strip search," he said. "Take it all off."

Ray looked down and shook his head. This was the worst of what they could do when they came to shake down the inmates. The regular guards rarely strip-searched the men on the row— there had to be a good reason. A weapon found somewhere or a big drug bust in general population. Usually, they left them alone, and the prisoners kept the peace. All the warden cared about on the row was keeping the peace. The inmates had representatives who met with the captain of the guards, and he told them what he needed and the men asked for what they needed. Usually, they met somewhere in the middle. The inmates didn't want trouble, and the guards were understaffed and didn't want trouble either.

But these were guards from another prison, and they liked busting in and flexing their muscle on death row. Ray had known guys like them his whole life. They were the guys in high school who felt powerless and picked on, and now they had some small bit of power in their little worlds.

"Strip!"

Ray took off all of his clothes, and they searched every inch and crevice of his body, just to humiliate him. He wondered what kind of men these were, who enjoyed doing something this degrading. It was a game for them. Ray wasn't a man to them—he didn't even think they thought of him as human.

"You can get dressed now. And clean this place up. We'll be here all shift. We might be back."

Everything was a mess. His sheets were in the dirt on the floor. Their boots had stepped on his clean clothes and maybe even on his toothbrush, which lay in the corner next to the toilet.

Tomorrow, the regular guards would come back and pretend to be shocked at what happened. They wouldn't mention that they had gone to one of the other prisons in Alabama and torn things up the same way. This is how they kept themselves from being accountable. *He threw out your picture of your mama? You got to be kidding me!*

And that's how it worked with a shakedown. You never saw it coming, and no one was ever responsible.

Alan Black filed an amended Rule 32 petition in 1994. That required the State to turn over all of their records and evidence to him for Ray's appeal.

In May 1997, Henry got his execution date. June 6. Ray and the others tried to keep it positive.

"Hold your head up, Henry."

"You just never know what's going to happen."

"The governor could give you a stay."

"Be positive."

Guys said these kinds of things to him in the yard, on the way to the shower. Ray thought Henry felt more love from the Black men on death row than he ever did at a KKK meeting or from his own father and mother.

The book club had met a few more times and read *Your Blues Ain't Like Mine*, *To Kill a Mockingbird*, and *Uncle Tom's Cabin*. All the books talked about race in the South, and Henry at first had shied away from the subject, almost pretending not to know how unfairly Black people were treated until they called him out on it. He was ashamed of how he had been brought up and ashamed of the beliefs that had brought him to the row. "You never knew what a person could grow up to become," he'd say. "Why tell someone she can't be a nurse or a guy he can't be a doctor or a lawyer because they're Black? That person could discover a cure for AIDS or for cancer. You just never know."

Ray knew he was thinking of Michael Donald, the boy he had killed. He knew Henry wondered what that boy might have grown up to become. Henry was the first white man to be put to death for killing a Black person in almost eighty-five years. Henry's death meant something to people outside of the row. It was making a point about racism and justice and fairness like all the books they had been reading in book club, but to the inmates, it was a family member being killed.

The guards were extra nice the week before they killed someone. Asking how they were and what they could get them. The condemned man could have visitors anytime he wanted, without any paperwork or hoops to jump through. He got something cold to drink and food from the vending machine or made special for you in the kitchen. Special treatment on the way to the death room.

Before Henry was moved to the death room to wait for his execution, he and Ray talked one last time.

"I'm sorry, Ray; I'm sorry for what I done."

"I know you are. God knows you are."

"I don't know if I ever told you this, but I have a brother named Ray. He's my brother too." It would probably seem unimaginable to a lot of people, but there it was: Henry considered Ray his brother.

Ray could hear that Henry was crying, and his heart broke for him. There was no past and no future on the row. You only had the moment you were in, and when you tried to survive moment to moment, there wasn't the luxury of judgment. Unbelievable as it might have seemed, Henry was Ray's friend. It wasn't complicated. Ray would show him compassion, because that's how he was raised. That's how he could lay his head down at night in this hellhole and feel like he could make it through another day. A laugh here and there. A helping hand. Friendship. Compassion for another human who was suffering. Ray would keep his humanity. They would not take that from him, no matter what.

At a few minutes before midnight on June 5, Ray stood at the door of his cell. He took off his shoe and started banging on the bars and wire. He wanted Henry to hear him. He wanted Henry to know he wasn't alone. Ray knew when they shaved Henry's head, and he heard when the generator kicked on. Ray banged louder, as did all of the other guys. They banged on their bars for Henry Hays. Black. White. It didn't matter. Henry was scared and alone. Ray knew that he was afraid that hell waited on the other side of death row because of what he had done. The inmates banged and yelled and hollered as loud as they could. For fifteen minutes, Ray screamed until his throat was raw and hoarse. He screamed so Henry would know that he meant something. He screamed so that whoever was there to watch the State of Alabama kill in their name knew that they were real men and that they could not be covered with a black hood and killed without feeling pain. Ray screamed because he knew that innocent men had been strapped into that horrid yellow chair, their dignity stripped away little by little, their worth as humans tied up with electric wires and thrown away like garbage. Innocent men had died in that chair. Guilty men had died in that chair. Strong men had wept like babies, and weak men had held steady as they met their deaths. Ray yelled for Henry so he would hear and know that he didn't have to meet his maker alone. And that whoever stared at him in that death chamber with cold eyes was no match against the heat of the inmates' cries. They screamed in protest and they screamed in unity and they screamed because there are times when screaming is all there is left to do.

You can't watch a man die—see how one day he is there and the next he is gone—and not think about your own death. Alan Black hadn't been back to see Ray, but Ray had received legal papers when Alan amended his petition again. By this point, Alan had been working on his case for over seven years. Ray was grateful to him. When Ray received word Alan was coming for a visit, he hoped it was good news.

"Ray, I got good news," he said. "I'm working on a deal. I think I've got the State to the point where they will consider life without parole. I'm pretty sure we can get you off death row."

He actually smiled at Ray when he said that. Like Ray was supposed to pat him on the back and be happy for that.

His name was Anthony Ray Hinton. People called him Ray.

"But I don't want life without parole," said Ray. "I'm innocent. I can't get life without parole. That's like admitting I did something that I didn't do." Ray had really thought Alan believed in him, that he knew Ray was innocent.

"It's a way to save your life, Ray. It's a great solution."

Ray stared at him for a good five minutes. "No," he said quietly.

"What?" he asked. "No, what?"

"I'm not going to agree to that. If I get life without parole, I have no way of walking free. I can't prove my innocence if I agree to life without parole. I'm not going to spend my life in prison."

"Ray, they're going to kill you. They're not going to let you go free. They don't care if you're innocent. They don't have any reason to rule in your favor. The judge has given money for experts now because they don't allow you to appeal for anything you could have appealed on before. They are denying everything we're claiming. Life without parole is a good option."

"What about the experts? What about the bullets?"

Alan Black just stared at Ray like he was an idiot. "I need money," he said. "I need $10,000."

"I don't have any money." Ray couldn't believe they were

back to this again. "You do know that I'm in here for robbing people. Why do you lawyers seem to think I have money? Ask Bryan Stevenson if you need money. He's the one who sent you. I don't have any money, and neither does my mama," he said. "She's been sick. Don't go bothering her for money."

"You need to ask at your church for the money. With $10,000, I can get you life without parole. Your church needs to collect the money. They're nice people; they're going to do that to save your life. Nobody wants to see you die, Ray. Not your mama, not me, not Bryan Stevenson, not your friends and your family, and not your church. Nobody wants that for you." He was pleading his case.

Ray got up. It wasn't just about the money.

It was about his innocence.

"I want to thank you for your time and for your help, but I won't be needing your services anymore."

Alan Black's mouth fell open, and he laughed a little. "What are you talking about, Ray?"

"I won't be needing your services any longer. You're not my attorney. I'm firing you."

"You're firing me?"

"Yes, I'm firing you. Thank you for everything up until now, but I'd rather die for the truth than live a lie. I'm not agreeing to life without parole. I'll rot and die in here before I agree to that. But thank you for working so hard."

Ray waved to the guard and walked out of the visiting area. He didn't look back at Alan Black, so he didn't know if he was still sitting there with his mouth hanging open or if he had gotten up to try to follow him. Ray didn't care. Alan Black didn't believe in him, and Ray didn't believe in Alan Black.

Some things, like the horrible strip searches, Ray had no choice about.

But he wasn't going to let anybody else shake him down.

Ray wasn't ready to give up on his life. He was going to walk out of that place as an innocent man, or he was going to die trying. Nothing more and nothing less.

Chapter Seventeen
GOD'S BEST LAWYER

"We have a choice. We can embrace our humanness, which means embracing our broken natures and the compassion that remains our best hope for healing. Or we can deny our brokenness, forswear compassion, and, as a result, deny our humanity."

—**Bryan Stevenson,** *Just Mercy*

"It would take me a long time to understand how systems inflict pain and hardship in people's lives and to learn that being kind in an unjust system is not enough."

—**Sister Helen Prejean,** *Dead Man Walking: An Eyewitness Account of the Death Penalty in the United States*

After firing Alan Black, Ray felt alone again—*really* alone. What should he do now?

Where could he turn? There was a bad joke that ran up and down the row, with guys repeating it all the time:

"What does capital punishment mean?"

"It means a guy without capital gets punished."

It wasn't funny, but it was true. It felt even truer now that he officially didn't have an attorney working on his appeal. He wondered how soon it would be before the courts found out he wasn't represented. Ray feared getting an execution date more than anything else. He asked one of the guards as he was making rounds if he could get Ray a phone number.

"What number you need?" he asked.

Honey, not vinegar. "I need to talk to your wife," joked Ray. "She is sending you to work with some suspicious-looking lunch meat, and I want to ask her why she's trying to kill you. I'm trying to save your life."

The guard laughed. "Who you trying to call? I have the Yellow Pages in the office."

"I would appreciate it if you could get me the number and the address for the Equal Justice Initiative in Montgomery."

He cocked his head to the side and stared at Ray for a moment. "You trying to get ahold of Bryan Stevenson?"

Ray nodded.

The guard smiled at him. "I hope that works out for you, Ray, I do. You're not like the other guys in here."

"We're all the same in here."

"Not in my opinion. I have his number; I'll bring it to you later on." He walked on, and Ray sat down on his bed to write a letter.

Hello, Mr. Stevenson,

My name is Anthony Ray Hinton, and I'm on Alabama death row. I would like to thank you for the lawyer from Boston; as you most likely know by now, it didn't work out. I know you're probably wanting to send a new lawyer, but I would like for you to be my lawyer. Please read his transcript, and if you can find one thing that points to my guilt, then don't worry about being my lawyer. I will take the punishment that Alabama is seeking. I don't have any money to pay you for your time, but if you would come see me, I can pay you for your gas.

I am an innocent man. I would never kill anyone. I hope to hear from you soon. May the God who made us all, continue to bless us all.

Sincerely, Ray Hinton, Z468

When the guard brought him the address and phone number later that night, Ray put the letter in an envelope and carefully wrote out the address across the front. He left his letter unsealed and wrote "Legal Correspondence" on the front. He knew the guards would read it anyway. They read everything.

The next day when it was time to go on the yard, Ray went to use the phone instead. He called Equal Justice Initiative—or EJI as it was called, for short—collect. He wanted to make sure that his letter was read. A woman answered, and Ray waited while the recording told her it was an inmate calling collect from Holman Prison. She accepted the charges.

"I'd like to speak to Bryan Stevenson," Ray said. "This is Anthony Ray Hinton from down at Holman, death row."

He heard a smile in her voice. "Why, nice to meet you, Mr. Hinton. Please hold and I will get Mr. Stevenson on the line."

Some generic hold music started playing, and Ray wondered how much it cost EJI to put collect calls on hold. He waited a few minutes, and then a man's voice came on the line.

"This is Bryan Stevenson." He sounded rushed and hurried.

"Hello, Mr. Stevenson. This is Anthony Ray Hinton from Holman. Death row."

"Hello?" he said; it sounded like a question.

"I wanted to thank you for sending Alan Black, but I wanted to let you know that I had to fire him."

There was silence on the other end. It stretched out for what felt like minutes.

"You fired him?"

"Yes, sir. I had to fire him. He asked me for $10,000. He wanted me to get my church to get him money. I don't have that kind of money."

"I'm so sorry, Mr. Hinton. Let me call him and talk to him."

"I sent you a letter; I need you to read that letter. I don't want Alan Black to be my attorney. He was trying to get me life without parole. I can't do that. Do you understand? Will you read my letter?" Ray knew he only had a little bit of time before the phone cut off, so he was rushing his words.

"Let me talk to him, and I will get word to you. We'll figure this out. We'll figure out something," he said. His voice sounded sincere, but Ray had been down this road with attorneys before.

"Just promise me you'll read my letter and consider it."

"Of course. I promise."

Months later, Ray received word that he had a legal visit.

He walked slowly to the visiting area, and seated at a table was a Black man, bald, who looked a bit younger than Ray. He was dressed in a suit and tie. Ray walked up to him, and he stood and gave Ray a wide smile.

"Mr. Hinton, I'm Bryan Stevenson." He held out his hand to shake, and when Ray lifted his arm to extend his own hand, it almost felt like he was moving in slow motion.

"Mr. Stevenson, it's nice to meet you," Ray said.

They shook hands, and in that moment, Ray felt a strength

and a compassion and a hope so big it seemed to shoot out of Stevenson's hand and into Ray's.

It was almost like an electric shock, and Ray gave him his best strong handshake back. Bryan Stevenson looked smart. He also looked tired. There were lines around his eyes and a sort of sadness hidden in the creases.

Ray sat down at the table and looked into Bryan Stevenson's eyes, and it felt like he could take a deep breath for the first time in over twelve years. There are some people you meet and you know they are going to change your life forever. Meeting Bryan Stevenson was like that for Ray.

"How are you?" Ray asked.

"Well, I'm fine, thank you. How are you, Mr. Hinton? Everything going okay for you here? Any problems?"

"You can call me Ray," Ray said.

"All right, then. You can call me Bryan."

"Thank you for coming to see me. It means a lot to me. I know you do a lot for the guys around here."

He nodded.

"I talked to Alan Black. I'm sorry about that."

"Are you going to be my attorney?" Ray asked. "Is that why you're here?"

"Right now, I'm just here to meet you and get to know you. Just talk for a bit. I'd like to hear about your case and your trial and your family."

He smiled, and Ray felt that same hope bloom in his heart.

Bryan Stevenson was sent by God.

"You know, when I was convicted, I told that courtroom that someday God was going to open my case again."

"Did you?"

"Yes, I did. But I didn't know it was going to take so long. I've been here almost twelve years. I can't even believe I've been here so long. It's been hell. I can't even tell you the kind of hell it's been."

Bryan looked into his eyes, and Ray saw that he knew. He understood. He had been to executions here. He had lost people too.

"But today is a good day. Because today, God sent me his best lawyer. Today is the day that God opened up my case."

Bryan laughed. And then he got quiet and said, "Tell me what happened."

"I'm innocent. I've never been violent in my life." Ray took a deep breath and continued. He needed this man. He needed this lawyer on his side. Ray knew that more than he had ever known anything. He *needed* Bryan Stevenson to believe he was innocent. "I made some mistakes. I drove off in a car that didn't belong to me. I wrote some bad checks, but I wrote them in my own name. I've made some mistakes. Sometimes I think God's punishing me for those mistakes, and other times I think God's got another plan for me, and that's why I'm here. I have a mother that loves me. She loves me more than any human deserves to be loved. Unconditionally. Do you know what that's like? Unconditional love? Not many guys here know that kind of love. A lot of them grew up without any kind of love at all. That hurts a man. It breaks him. It breaks him in ways that no person should be broken. You know what I mean?"

"I do." Bryan looked sad, but he was nodding at Ray.

It all came out in a rush. "I was at work. I didn't try to rob and kill anyone. I was at work where a guard had to clock me in and clock me out. They told me it didn't matter that it wasn't me. They told me that a white man was going to say that I did it and that's all it would take. I was going to be guilty because I was going to have a white jury and a white judge and a white prosecutor. My defense attorney wasn't paid nothing. He couldn't get money for an expert. They took my mom's gun and said it was the gun that killed those men. My mom's gun hadn't been fired in twenty-five years. His expert only had one eye. I cried when he got off the stand. I knew they were going to find me guilty, but I didn't do it. People lied and I've never hurt anyone in my life. A man called during the trial and said he was the one, but my attorney was mad he woke him up. That guy knew things. I didn't know anything. I'd never hurt anyone. I didn't do it. I'm innocent and they have me in here and I can't get out. I'm suffocating in here."

Bryan just sat there and listened to every word.

"They're killing people. They're killing people right next to me. *I have to smell my friends as they burn.* Do you understand? I have to breathe in their death and it never leaves and they smile at you but someday they're going to come for me too and I am innocent. I need to get home to my mom. She's not feeling good. She doesn't come to visit anymore, and she needs me at home. I need to go back home. I'm innocent. I can't get out of here, and I'm innocent."

Ray didn't feel any doubt coming off Bryan. He looked Ray in the eye the whole time. He asked questions about his mom and about other family. Ray told him about Lester and how for twelve years he had come to see Ray every visiting day. Never missed a day. That was true friendship, and Ray told Bryan that he wished everyone had a best friend like Lester. Bryan asked about his trial and who had testified at his sentencing. He seemed surprised that Perhacs hadn't put Lester or his mom or anybody from church on the stand when Ray was sentenced. He asked Ray some questions about work and had Ray walk him through clocking in the night of the Smotherman incident.

They talked for over two hours. Ray felt comfortable with this man. He asked Bryan if he was an Auburn fan and Ray told him that Alan Black was a Red Sox fan and he should have known then it would never work out between them. Ray told Bryan that after he got Ray out of there, they could go to a Yankees game.

Bryan laughed. Ray asked him about his work. Did he have any family? He told Bryan funny stories about the guards, and about book club and how the warden was shutting them down because some of the other guys were saying it wasn't fair that they got to go out to book club and that either everyone goes or no one goes.

Ray told him they needed some fans on death row, that it was too hot in the summer to even breathe right.

Bryan Stevenson listened to everything Ray said. He didn't seem in a rush to finish. He didn't interrupt. He just listened.

It was a powerful thing to be listened to like that.

"I have an idea about my case," Ray said.

"What is it?" Bryan asked. He leaned in, like he was really interested.

"Well, I don't know if you're an attorney who doesn't like it if your client has ideas—" Ray didn't want to offend him or put him off.

"Ray," he interrupted. "I want to hear every idea you have. We are a team. Along with my staff at EJI, we're going to do everything we can. I want to know what you're thinking every step of the way. I'm going to review your transcript closely. Any idea you have is important to me. No matter what it is."

Ray smiled. This was what he wanted to hear. "I want you to get a ballistics expert."

"Yes, we're going to do that; I think Alan got someone."

"I need you to get the best ballistics expert there is. The judges here are so biased. It can't be a woman. It can't be someone from up North. It has to be a man, preferably a white, Southern man. He needs to believe in the death penalty. He needs to be the best of the best, the guy who taught the State's guys. He needs to have every reason in the world to want to see me die if I'm guilty, but he has to be honest. As long as he's an honest, racist, Southern, white expert, I'll be okay."

Bryan laughed. "I can see your point. That's a good idea. We'll look into it. I know someone from the FBI. I think we want to get more than one expert, but let me review your file. Let me see the reports from the State's experts. Let me see what your expert said and did. I need to get up to speed on everything, and then I'll come back to see you. Okay?"

They shook hands again, and their eyes locked as they said goodbye. He didn't promise then he was going to get Ray out of there, but Ray saw it in his eyes. Ray saw the promise that he would make later. It was a promise Ray would hold on to through a lot of dark nights.

The guard walked Ray back to his cell, and as soon as the door shut behind him, he dropped to his knees. He folded his hands and bowed his head.

Thank you, God. Thank you for sending Bryan Stevenson. I trust things to happen in your time, so I'm not going to ask you why you didn't send him earlier. Please, God, watch over Bryan Stevenson. Take care of him, because he's doing your work. God, bless the men on death row. Bless my mom, and please put hope in her heart that her baby's coming home. I'm going to tell her you sent your best lawyer to me. God, please keep her in good health. Please, God, let the truth come out. Thank you, God. I know you've sent your best lawyer, and I know you've reopened my case.

Ray finished his prayer just as the first sob broke loose from his chest. He spent the next two hours on his knees sobbing like a baby.

Some nights were just made for crying.

Chapter Eighteen
BULLET PROOF

"Standing alone, the evidence in this case was simply insufficient to prove Mr. Hinton's guilt."
—Bryan Stevenson, opposition to State's proposed order, 2002

Ray's mom wanted to cook for Bryan Stevenson. It was the way she showed love, and after Ray told her about him, all she wanted to do was show her love.

"He's going to be coming to talk to you," Ray told her.

"Well, what does he like to eat?" she asked. "I want to make him something special. You find out what his favorite meal is, and I'll fix it right up. I'd like to give him some money also."

"No, Mama. You can't give him money. He won't take it. Please don't try to give him money."

"Well, what does he say? When are you going to come home, baby? I'm ready for you to come home now."

He always caught his breath when she said that. It was too hard for her to visit, the drive was too rough, so she hadn't seen Ray in a long time. And he knew she was sick, in the way you know things about the people you love, but no one had said it out loud. He knew they didn't want him to worry, and so Ray just went along with it and pretended things were okay. It seemed easier that way; he couldn't be home to take care of her, and the pain of that fact was too much to face. He was a prisoner. It shouldn't have been so hard for an innocent man to get out of prison, but it was.

There is a point in a struggle where you have to surrender. You have to stop trying to swim upstream, stop fighting the current. Ray hadn't given up the idea of walking out of prison, but he couldn't fight it every single day and survive. He had to make a home of Holman to survive. He had to block out his real home and block out the outside world. It didn't matter anymore what other people did at 10:00 a.m. every day. For Ray, in his home on the row, 10:00 a.m. was lunchtime. He had to accept that. He had to face the fact that in his home, men cried and screamed and moaned every day, all day. In his home, the rats and the roaches were free to come and go as they pleased, while Ray was not. In his home, people could come in at any time and turn his home upside down, and he had to take it. He had to say, "Yes, sir," and "Thank you, sir," in order to live. In his home, death was always at his door. It circled his house, watching and waiting and always present. Ray survived in his home mostly week to week—between visits with Lester, but sometimes it was minute to minute and hour to hour. In his home, he always knew when his family would die. In the real world, Ray didn't know that death stalked the ones he loved as well. Ray couldn't face that reality. He couldn't live in the real world—only in the world of his imagination and the world that existed in his cell.

"It's going to take some time, Mama," he said. "He has to undo what the other lawyers did. It's like he's starting over. But he promised me he was going to get me out of here. He knows I'm innocent, Mama; he believes me. He's proven it."

"Of course you're innocent. No child of mine would ever hurt someone. I didn't like how that other attorney used your

name. He didn't do right by you. I don't think he believed in
you."

She was talking about McGregor. It was hard for Ray to hear
how confused she got at times. Lester told Ray she was fine, just
got tired easily and it pained her to sit in a car for seven hours
in one day, which Ray understood. His mom still came to visit,
but only every few months or so. They were getting older. They
were all getting older.

After Bryan had come to visit, Ray received a letter from him.

November 1, 1998

*Anthony Ray Hinton, Z-468 Holman State Prison Holman, 3700
Atmore, Alabama 36503*

Dear Ray:

*We have reviewed the trial transcript of your case and
prepared a case summary. We are now organizing the
investigation. I am sending you a copy of the trial summary
and would like you to review it. I will want to talk to you
again about some of the evidence presented against you at
trial, and it may be useful for you to refresh your recollection
by reviewing the trial summary.*

*I hope you are well. We are starting to make some progress
in identifying areas where there may be a basis for moving
your case in the right direction. I will be down to see you in
the next couple of weeks. Hang in there.*

Sincerely,
Bryan Stevenson

Bryan did visit Ray a few weeks later, and a few weeks after that, and on a regular basis. They got to know each other, and for parts of the visit Bryan was his attorney, and for other parts he was Ray's friend. Sometimes they would go an hour or more not talking about his case. Instead, they would talk about the weather in Alabama, the college football season, food they liked and food they hated.

Some days, Ray could see Bryan was tired, and he wondered about the wear on a person when so many lives depend on what you do each day. Bryan carried a big burden, and it wasn't just Ray's. He spoke of justice and of mercy and of a system that was so broken it locked up children and the mentally ill and the innocent. "No one is beyond redemption," he would say. No one is undeserving of their own life or their own potential to change. He had such compassion for victims and for perpetrators, and an intolerance and even anger for those in power who abused that power. Bryan Stevenson was not happy with McGregor, and he wasn't happy with Perhacs either. Ray learned Bryan had a team of young lawyers working for him and volunteering to fight the good fight, and joked that those not at the top of the class might help.

"You might want to bring in some of those C students," Ray said. "Those middle-of-the-class students sometimes know how to work the system. They have some hustle to them."

Ray liked making him laugh. Bryan wore his work and his passion for his work on his face, but sometimes Ray could see it fall away and they were just two guys talking about regular stuff, like football and politics and good barbecue and guys they knew who could act the fool. In those moments, Ray wasn't condemned, and Bryan wasn't a lawyer. They were just Ray and

Bryan, more alike than different. They both knew Ray's life was in Bryan's hands—but that was a burden they had to set aside now and then. It was a relief to know Bryan truly believed in Ray's innocence. There was no talk of life without parole. Ray was innocent, and Bryan was going to yell and argue and fight until the State agreed to acknowledge it had made a mistake.

Ray hoped it would be soon. He prayed it would be soon.

Hope can be a four-letter word in prison. It can tease a man by staying close but just out of reach. Ray had hope. He had lots of hope. But his life was passing him by quickly, and every year, he grieved for the year he'd lost. Ray was grateful to not be executed, but it was like existing in limbo—floating somewhere between life and death and never knowing where he was going to land.

The original case summary Bryan prepared was almost two hundred pages long. Ray liked that Bryan wanted him to review it. He liked that Bryan asked his opinion. He liked finally feeling that he had a voice in his own defense.

When Bryan wrote, he always told Ray to "hang in there," and from Bryan, those words weren't throwaway words. They weren't just a way to end a letter or a phone call. They both knew a lot of guys on the row—eleven, to be exact, since Ray was there—who'd chosen not to hang in there. Giving up was always a temptation. Sometimes, taking his own life almost seemed like a better choice than letting the State take it from him. Ray was not going to take his own life, but he always appreciated Bryan's telling him to hang in there. It got Ray through another day. Another long night. Ray took comfort in Bryan's letters and visits. Bryan was truly working for him, and Ray prayed for him each and every night.

Bryan found two good old boy experts from Texas and another from the FBI. They were the best of the best in the country. They usually only testified for the prosecutors in a case. They were white. They were honest. They had credentials that made Higgins and Yates look like hacks. They were unimpeachable, as Bryan liked to say.

Ray had gotten word from the guard that Bryan wanted to talk to him and he should call him right away. Bryan had an understanding with the guards that he could call them and they would give Ray a message to call him collect. Sometimes it seemed like the guards wanted to see Ray leave death row just as much as he did.

"Ray, I have good news." Bryan's voice sounded excited.

"What's that?"

"I got the reports from Emanuel, Cooper, and Dillon. Their report says that none of the bullets from all three locations match your mother's gun. They also said that the recovered bullets and the test bullets do not match. We also found out that Higgins and Yates had worksheets that the State didn't turn over to your attorney. Their worksheets showed question marks and missing information. They didn't follow proper procedures, and they didn't record any land or groove information for any of the six bullets. We can prove this. We can prove that the only evidence against you is false. There's no way the bullets match your mother's gun."

Ray took a deep breath. Finally! "So what do we do now?" he asked. "When can I get out of here?" He was ready to pack it up right then and there. "Come pick me up, Bryan; I'm ready to go home!"

"Well, it's usual for experts to meet and review the tests together when they have conflicting results. It's a professional courtesy and part of their procedure according to their code of ethics. Emanuel, Cooper, and Dillon will have to meet with Higgins and Yates. It's a process, Ray, but we're on the right track. I'm going to make sure they understand there's a problem with your case. The ballistics are all they have; without that, they have no conviction. They said that in your trial. They conceded that fact."

"Thank you," Ray said. "Bryan, I can't tell you enough how grateful I am to you." He started to choke up.

"We're not home yet, Ray, but we're on our way."

"I'll be here," Ray said. "You just let me know when it's time to go home."

"I'll get you home, Ray. I promise you."

Bryan's next letter explained that he was working on getting Ray's conviction and sentence vacated, which meant they would be declared legally void and be overturned. He added

If Jefferson County concedes that mistaken ballistics evidence means that you are innocent, we would probably then agree to have the weapon tested by some government agency, perhaps the ATF or the FBI. Assuming those test results come back the right way, we would then ask for a declaration of innocence.

Bryan was also working on getting more media coverage of Ray's case, preparing to take their story of injustice to *60 Minutes*, the award-winning, internationally known news program. He ended his letter, as he always did, with encouragement.

Anyway, things are going well for the case. Keep your head up, something may be soon to break. I'm enclosing some

money to help you out. Let me know if you need anything
else. I'll see you soon, my friend.

Sincerely,
Bryan Stevenson

Ray read the letter and the attached memo that Bryan sent with it. The memo began in bold type:

THE ANTHONY RAY HINTON CASE

Anthony Ray Hinton has been on Alabama's death row for
sixteen years for crimes he did not commit.

It went on to detail the newly discovered ballistics findings and his confirmed alibi of being at work at Bruno's; it listed the mistaken previous ballistics evidence; and it recounted how the police had pressured other employees at Food World to say they saw Ray there that night, and how they had refused and said they didn't see him there. Only Clark Hayes, the grocery clerk, said he saw Ray there, and he was pressured just like the others. It also brought up Ray's polygraph. The polygraph nobody wanted to look at.

Ray held up the money order Bryan had sent with his letter. He was still amazed at how selfless Bryan was. Not only didn't he shake Ray down, he sent cards and money for Ray's commissary purchases. The hearing was scheduled for March, and Ray went to bed thinking about that hearing. *They will have to let me go, then. I am innocent. The FBI expert had even said so.*

The more Bryan uncovered, though, the more it seemed like this wasn't just an innocent mistake. To let Ray go, Alabama was going to have to admit they purposely sent him to death row. The police had coerced witnesses into saying he was at Food World. The detectives had given Ray's name to Smotherman before he'd identified him from a photo that had his initials on it. Ray could feel the rage building again—the white-hot hate of anger at how much they had stolen of his life. Sixteen years. How much more could a man take? *How did Reggie sleep at night, knowing he had sent me to my death?* Every day, he had to keep reminding himself that he still mattered. Alabama had made a mistake.

Ray was innocent. And finally he could prove it.

Ray read Bryan's letter and the memo over and over again, and that night, he prayed harder than he had ever prayed before. The truth was shining a light so big that they couldn't ignore it. Ray prayed for Judge Garrett and for McGregor and for Higgins and Yates. He prayed for Perhacs. Bryan had told Ray that Perhacs and McGregor were friends. He also told Ray that Bob McGregor had a history of racial bias and was twice found guilty of illegally discriminating against African Americans in jury selections, once in Mobile and another time in Jefferson County.

Ray hadn't known any of this, but still, he forgave Perhacs for not telling him he was friends with McGregor. Ray also blamed himself in some ways; he thought he'd been young and stupid and so trusting of a system that was rigged against him from the start. Ray prayed he could forgive himself as well.

He prayed for Bryan's voice to be the voice of reason, and for fairness and justice. But Ray never forgot that Bryan was a Black man too, just like Ray. And he was up against the same ignorance Ray was up against. He was smarter than them all, though. And God was on his side.

That much he knew.

His mama had taught him well.

God had a plan, and God was always on the side of justice. God could do everything but fail. Ray had to believe. Sixteen long years. He was ready for God's justice and mercy. His freedom was so close he could taste it and feel it, and sometimes at night, he would be back in his mama's yard on a hot day in July, cutting the grass and thinking about going to church. He would wake up and realize this had all been a bad dream. All a dream. He had not spent sixteen years of his life on death row. In his dream, he'd walk into the kitchen and lay his head on his mama's shoulder, and she would pat his back like she always did when he had a bad dream.

This nightmare wasn't real. He had his whole life in front of him, and his mama was there telling him everything was going to be okay.

It was only a nightmare. It wasn't real.

How could any of it have been real?

Chapter Nineteen
EMPTY CHAIRS

*"You think your pain and your heartbreak are unprecedented in
the history of the world, but then you read."*

—James Baldwin

Right before Ray was supposed to have his Rule 32 hearing,
the State's attorney general's office filed what's called a
writ of mandamus to force the lower court to dismiss his petition altogether. Basically, that meant they didn't want the lower
court to look at the evidence of his innocence. Their motion to
dismiss said that they were not required to listen to or defend
any of his innocence claims or look at the new ballistics tests
because too much time had passed, or there wasn't any "new"
evidence. Ray couldn't believe it. They said it was a waste of
time. The attorney general said in his brief that Ray should
be blocked from establishing his innocence because it would
"waste three days or two days of taxpayer money." They weren't
even willing to hear him out. To look at the new evidence. To
see what Perhacs had failed to show them in 1986. It hurt all
over again. What kind of a world was it where an innocent man
can lose sixteen years of his life and it's a waste of time to let
him prove he's innocent? Ray's sixteen years was less important
than a couple of days of the attorney general's time.

Bryan sent Ray a letter explaining everything and offering

encouragement. He was always there to make sure Ray's spirits never dropped too low at every legal twist and turn.

March 12, 2002

Anthony Ray Hinton, Z-468 Holman State Prison Holman, 3700
Atmore, Alabama 36503

Dear Ray:

I just wanted to touch base with you after what seems like a very strange five days. I spoke with Judge Garrett on Monday morning to try and block your transfer to Birmingham and to confirm that we would not litigate this case piecemeal. The judge is very angry at the State. I think he is even more suspicious of their desperation to keep us from presenting this evidence than I had hoped. The State may have made a serious mistake in antagonizing the court this way. The State waited until the day before the hearing to file a stay motion, which is pretty bad form, if nothing else.

We will file a response to the State's papers in the next two weeks. The State is essentially arguing that our evidence will be the same as what was presented at trial and therefore we have no right to present it. We are saying that they can't know what the evidence is until we present it and if it's unpersuasive then they have nothing to fear. The appeal likely means that it will be May before we can schedule another hearing date.

We had a very good week last week and had organized a pretty compelling case. I'll talk to you about some recent developments, new witnesses we found, when I see you next at the prison. I will try to get down as soon as I can.

I know it's upsetting to have the hearing postponed like this. I was pretty furious all day on Saturday. We had spent lots of money on nonrefundable plane tickets for witnesses, rented computer equipment for audiovisual presentations for the courtroom, and done a lot of stuff to prepare for this hearing. Most importantly, however, it's just wrong for you to spend more days and weeks on death row for something you did not do.

However, our day will come. Don't be too discouraged, the race is not given to the quick but to the one who endures. I'm more hopeful than ever that we will prevail and you will go home.

Enclosed is the State's motion, our initial response, and the court's order. I'm trying to schedule a time to see you sometime in the next few weeks. Hang in there, my friend.

Sincerely,
Bryan Stevenson

Ray wasn't surprised that the State was doing its best to keep him locked away and quiet. It was what the court had done from the beginning. It was still a lynching. It was taking decades to get the noose wrapped just right. On top of that, the State was unwilling to admit it had made a mistake. This system would rather accept injustice than admit that it had been unjust.

Ray knew that there were men before him and men after him who would abuse the system, who would be guilty but exhaust every claim to try to keep from getting killed. He didn't blame them. He *couldn't* blame them. Who wouldn't fight for their survival? For their right to live? And yes, Ray understood that the victims didn't have a chance to fight for their right to live. What he didn't understand was how *any* killing could be justified. Man didn't have the right to take a life. The State didn't have the right to take a life either. They were killing on behalf of the people, and Ray wondered what the people really believed. Yes, there were brutal, unremorseful, coldhearted, sociopathic, danger-to-society killers on death row. Ray knew this for a fact. He walked next to them on the yard. He showered with them, talked to them. He knew some of them would kill him in a heartbeat if they could—not that they hated him, but killing was what they did. Some had intellectual disabilities, and others would be considered geniuses. No matter what, Ray still didn't believe any person or any institution had a right to take their life, no matter what they had done.

"The people" was such a general term that Ray wondered what would happen if the prison asked the *real* people. "Jo Martin, we are going to kill Anthony Ray Hinton today, and we're going to do it in your name. We're going to say that we are killing him on behalf of Jo Martin. Is that okay?" Or Sarah Paulson, or Angela Ruiz, or Victor Wilson, or insert any name.

"The people" were made up of real people, and so were the condemned men on the row. Life is brutal, tragic, unbearable, and inhumane at times. Ray knew that the pain one man can cause another was limitless, but he didn't see—he *couldn't* see—how creating more pain made anything better. When you took a life, it didn't bring back a life. It didn't undo what was done. It wasn't logical. This was just creating an endless chain of death and killing. It was barbaric. No baby is born a murderer. No toddler dreams of being on death row someday. Every killer on death row was taught to be a killer—by parents, by a system, by the brutality of another brutalized person—but no one was born a killer. His friend Henry wasn't born to hate. He was taught to hate, and to hate so much that killing was justified. No one was born to this one precious life to be locked in a cell and murdered. Not the innocent like Ray, but not the guilty either. Life was a gift given by God. He believed it should and could only be taken by God as well. Or whatever a man believed in. It didn't matter to him. But God never gave the guards, or the warden, or the judges, or the State of Alabama, or the federal government, or the people the right to take a life.

Nobody had that right.

Ray was afraid every single day on death row. And he also found a way to find joy every single day. He learned that fear and joy are both a choice. And every morning when he opened his eyes at 3:00 a.m. and saw the cement and the mesh wire and the sadness and the filth of his tiny cell, Ray had a choice. Would he choose fear, or would he choose love? Would he choose a prison, or would he choose a home? It wasn't always easy. On the days that Ray chose a home, he could laugh with the guards, listen to the other guys, talk about their cases, about books and ideas and what they all might do when they walked out of their prison hell. But on the days when Ray opened his eyes and felt nothing but terror, when every corner of that cell looked like a black-and-white horror film with an ax-wielding killer just waiting to jump out at him and hack him to pieces, he would close his eyes again and he would leave.

Ray also had to give up his dreams of Halle Berry for Sandra

Bullock. He had seen the movie *Speed* and he thought Sandra would be good to have in case he ever busted out of death row and needed a getaway driver. He'd also watched her play a law student on a Black man's defense team, and her portrayal made Ray think she would fight for him. She would stand up to them all, and in his mind, she—along with Bryan—was Ray's voice out in the world.

In these fantasies, with Halle or Sandra or the Queen of England, all of them, Ray never imagined having children. He couldn't bear even the idea of being separated from his children. When the dreams were over, he had to leave Sandra, leave his mom, leave his professional baseball career, and travel back to death row and be there for a while. Ray didn't want to do that to a child. He knew how hard it was for him to be apart from his mom, and he wouldn't wish that pain on anyone, especially not a child.

The guys on the row who had children bore a pain that was almost too much to witness. They ached and they cried and they missed all the things that other parents take for granted. And they also knew how much their children suffered—no child wanted to brag about his or her dad on death row. Ray knew there were women on death row, a couple of hours away at Tutwiler Prison. He couldn't imagine the guards putting a woman to death. Especially a woman with children. But one of the guys on death row was a guy named George Sibley. He and his wife, Lynda, had both been sent to death row, and they had a nine-year-old son with them when they killed a police officer in 1993.

Lynda was executed before George. Ray wondered what it was like for a man to be locked in a cell and have his wife about to be murdered and not be able to do a thing about it?

On May 10, 2002, they brought her to Holman. They walked her through the row. A woman on death row. She wore white like the rest of the prisoners. She held her head up and looked straight ahead. They shaved her head just like they shaved a man's head. Ray didn't know if she and George got to see each other. George never spoke of that day. When she was executed, Ray and the others banged on the bars. They made some noise. For her. For George. For their son who was eighteen years old by that time. Ray felt physically ill even trying to put himself in George's shoes. He knew George wished he had gone first.

The guards who strapped her to the chair and then put her dead body on a gurney would finish those tasks and then hand George his breakfast a few hours later. They would smile and ask him how he was doing, but they would never be able to look him in the eye again. How could they?

Ray could not comprehend it.

Lynda was the last person to be electrocuted in Yellow Mama. After her execution, the prison began remodeling the death chamber and getting ready for a new way to kill.

It was called lethal injection.

Chapter Twenty

GOING HOME

"Approximately 40 percent of the 2,739 people currently on death row have spent at least 20 years awaiting execution, and 1 in 3 of these prisoners are older than 50."

—Slate.com, March 2013[23]

Ray walked into the Rule 32 hearing hopeful. Perhacs took the stand and admitted Payne as an expert had been a failure on his part. He told the court how he didn't have enough money to mount a defense or to pay for a qualified expert. The three new experts took the stand. They stated that there was no proof the bullets matched Ray's mom's gun.

Ray was glad to see Lester outside of the visiting yard. And his mom too. But it was also painful to see her. She looked frail and sick, and her hair was gone from places on her head. She looked at Ray and smiled a tired smile that made Ray want to run to her and hold her in his arms. That was his mama. And all he could do was take a deep breath and be grateful to see her at all. Their phone calls were few and far between, and they hurt too. She often got confused on the phone, and wasn't sure who she was even talking to. Phoebe, Lester's mom, was there too, and Ray soaked up her warm smile and reassuring

---

23 https://slate.com/news-and-politics/2017/03/for-many-death-row
-inmates-the-long-process-leading-to-capital-punishment-is-cruel.html

nod. Perhacs, on the other hand, barely acknowledged Ray's presence in the hearing. Ray could see that he had aged. Perhacs had talked to Bryan over the phone quite a bit, but when Bryan and another attorney went to meet with him in person in advance of the hearing, he had taken one look at Bryan and said, "I didn't know you had a tan." Apparently, Bryan had sounded "white" to Perhacs—whatever that was supposed to mean. Did it mean that he thought less of Bryan now, or more?

Ray wondered if Perhacs had ever cared that he held Ray's life in his hands. Ray thought Perhacs knew that he was innocent; he could see it in his eyes the few times Perhacs glanced his way. Did that keep him up at night? Did Perhacs and McGregor ever talk about him? Did they care at all, or was he just another Black boy who wasn't going quietly, a nuisance, but nothing to worry about?

McGregor wasn't at the hearing, but Ray didn't care one way or the other. His days of hating were over. Ray had forgiven McGregor. His sins were between him and God. Ray also forgave the rest of them. To Ray, they were a shameful lot of sad men, and he prayed for their souls.

Ray was innocent, and the three ballistics experts could not be argued with. He closed his eyes and imagined Garrett banging his gavel and standing up to yell, "In light of these three independent ballistics experts and in the name of true justice, I hereby declare Mr. Hinton innocent and order for him to be released immediately!"

That didn't happen.

There were three assistant attorneys general at the hearing. They had tried every which way to block the hearing from happening, but it was happening, and they didn't seem too happy about it.

Neither did the judge; Ray saw him yawn during the experts' testimony.

"What issues does the petitioner want to raise in the Rule 32 at this time?" asked Judge Garrett. Ray noticed Garrett never once looked at him—it was like Ray didn't exist.

Bryan stood up and explained that they planned to present the evidence of Ray's innocence. He added, "In our petition, we talk about prosecutorial misconduct with closing argument. The record speaks for itself on that issue."

Ray wondered what McGregor would've thought about that statement—prosecutorial misconduct. Maybe Perhacs would tell him.

Bryan went on, and Judge Garrett argued back, asking if Bryan was trying to present the same evidence, but using it with a different theory. He said they couldn't introduce evidence if it had already been considered by the courts.

Bryan didn't back down. "Our primary presentation is about the innocence claim and about the ineffectiveness of counsel claim and about claims flowing from due process violations relating to the withholding of exculpatory evidence. All those issues are cognizable in this Rule 32 process and cognizable by this court." He was saying that they wanted to present issues that were new and absolutely valid.

Score one for Bryan, thought Ray.

Bryan told Garrett he was going to present evidence from experts. Ray was amazed when Garrett played dumb about the evidence. Ray had been trying to get the court and the State to look at these new experts and their reports for years.

"Was there not evidence of both of those—by experts on both sides at trial?" Garrett looked at Bryan smugly.

"Well, Your Honor, I guess two things. We believe that the State was wrong, and we believe that Mr. Payne was not qualified to make the kind of examination that these experts are qualified to make."

"Well, that issue would be moot since that issue was raised in the trial of the case, wouldn't it?"

Ray sighed. *Why wouldn't they just look at the evidence?*

Bryan's voice rose. "No. We can present evidence that establishes that the State is wrong."

"What would be the nature of the testimony presented by your experts in this regard?"

Bryan stared at Garrett for a few seconds and then took a breath.

Give it to him, Bryan, Ray thought.

After Bryan explained that the new experts would show that the bullets used had not come from the same gun, and that meant that the State's insistence on Ray's mother's old gun as the sole weapon had to be wrong, Garrett interrupted him.

"Well, isn't this just a differing of experts, one expert disagreeing with another expert? Of course we had that at the trial of the case."

"No, Your Honor. I don't believe that's what this is."

"Are these the ultimate experts in the whole wide universe that are going to testify to that?"

"Yes, sir," said Bryan. "I believe they are."

"What if we come up with some different experts later on that are even more recognized as the ultimate experts? That's what we're getting into—a swearing contest between experts."

In that moment, Ray realized that the real killer could walk into this courtroom with pictures of himself committing the crime, and the judge wouldn't accept the evidence. The attorney general would just say, "That's an old story wrapped in a new cover." This wasn't about justice.

This system would rather accept injustice than admit that it had been unjust.

"Your Honor, I don't think that's our case. We have been trying, frankly, for the last eight years to have the State reexamine this evidence. We don't believe that anybody from the Department of Forensic Sciences can now look at this evidence and come in here and tell you that these bullets were fired from one weapon or that they were fired from the weapon recovered from Mr. Hinton . . .

"This is not a battle of experts. We would welcome any expert the State could identify that the court appoints to look at this evidence and disagree with our findings. We have three experts from different places, because we want to make it clear that this is not a battle of experts. We think any competent, trained expert that looks at this evidence now is going to come to the same conclusion about how these bullets were not fired from a single weapon. They were not fired from the weapon recovered from Mr. Hinton. That's our evidence."

Ray watched, amazed, as Assistant Attorney General James R. Houts argued with Bryan about Payne being a competent expert. Way back during Ray's trial, they called Payne all sorts of names—and expert wasn't one of them. Bryan argued that the new evidence established his innocence, and this made the evidence allowed in a Rule 32 proceeding.

Houts turned to the judge. "To the extent that Mr. Stevenson is attempting to make an actual innocence claim that is constitutional, the U.S. Supreme Court does not recognize actual innocence as a constitutional claim through which you can bring a habeas corpus action."

So apparently being convicted and sentenced to death even if actually innocent was not considered unconstitutional—unless there was a specific constitutional violation that could be identified from the trial. Ray knew a habeas corpus action was part of the federal appeals process that Bryan would begin if he lost in all the state courts. He didn't want to think about that. Bryan had told him the federal appeals process was extremely narrow and difficult.

Bryan cleared his throat. "I feel some need, Your Honor, to just kind of be real clear about what we're saying here. And I can't expect this court to do anything but hear me when I say this. But we believe this man is innocent—innocent—and that is why we think this evidence is so critical. And this is not like any standard Rule 32 case. It's not even like a standard death penalty case." Bryan finished up by saying, "We believe this evidence is compelling. We believe it's compelling and will be compelling to this court. We believe it ought to be compelling to the State. But we think we ought to have the right to present it."

Judge Garrett was silent for a minute and then asked, "What makes this evidence so different from that evidence which was presented at trial, except that it's by different persons?"

Bryan explained that it was rare to have three different experts separately find the same thing and even rarer that several people look at evidence, find the same thing, and that thing is not what was presented at trial. He also pointed out that no one from the State was prepared to prove a match now or say that they could find exactly what was found in 1985.

Bryan broke down his experts' qualifications. "What we have are experts or leaders in the association of firearms and tool mark examinations. Mr. Dillon was the head of the FBI in their unit for many years, its former past president for the Association of Firearm and Tool Mark Examiners. He's taught all over the country, consults with the FBI, consults with the ATF.

"Mr. Emanuel and Mr. Cooper work mostly for the prosecution. They've worked for the United States military, the State of Texas. They work for Dallas County prosecutors regularly. These experts have testified and examined over two thousand cases. They've been qualified over two hundred times. They're leaders in this field. And we've really spared no cost in getting the people we could identify as the best in the country, because we really wanted to make it clear to the court that this wasn't about a mere dispute but about a critical piece of factual evidence on which this conviction stands."

Ray thought that should have been enough for Garrett. Bryan had unimpeachable experts. Men who had every reason to find Ray guilty. Houts fought it the whole way. Garrett argued the State's side as well. But Bryan never faltered. Ray had never seen him like this. God's best lawyer was preaching the law at them like the law had never been preached at them before. Ray wished that he'd had Bryan on his case in 1985. If Bryan had represented him, Ray knew that he would never have gone to death row. He probably would have never even gone to trial. It wasn't fair that justice could be so arbitrary and the truth so hard for the State to admit.

Bryan kept fighting; he didn't back down an inch. "What we're saying, Your Honor, is that the State made a mistake. It's a 'made a mistake' case. And what I hear the State to be arguing is that it's too late. If they made a mistake, you can't do anything about it." He pointed out that the court was basically shrugging off the evidence of Ray's innocence, the strength of his arguments, everything, in favor of just moving forward with execution. "What I'm saying is that that's not what the law says, and it would be an unconscionable result. They made a mistake, and we think we can show that."

They argued back and forth until lunch. The State didn't think any of Ray's claims should be allowed to be presented at this hearing. They just wanted Bryan to shut up and for Ray to go to the death chamber. Bryan persisted, and ultimately Garrett let the hearing happen, and Bryan was allowed to present all of the evidence and witnesses.

The State didn't defend the fact that Bryan found worksheets that Higgins and Yates and McGregor hadn't turned over to Perhacs that illustrated how flimsy their case had been. They didn't defend any of it. They didn't think that they needed to test the bullets or the gun again. In their mind, none of this was allowed because it was too late or it didn't count as new evidence based on their obscure interpretation of the rules of appeal.

Ray wondered how proof of innocence could ever be disregarded. *Who are we if we allow that? What part of our system is working if an innocent man can be killed and no one cares because of rules that were made to be able to kill him quickly?* It was like it was some kind of game for them. The clock was ticking. *Prove your innocence in five, four, three, two, one . . . too late now . . . off with your head!*

Ray was taken back to Holman after the hearing. He'd seen and heard Bryan be absolutely brilliant in court, but Ray saw that it was like he was talking to a wall. The prosecutors, the judge, the State wanted Ray dead. It didn't matter; guilty or innocent, they just wanted to kill him.

Chapter Twenty-One

HOMEGOING

"There has never been, nor will there ever be, anything quite so special as the love between the mother and a son."

—Source Unknown

Ray hadn't been able to say anything to his mom or Lester before he was taken away from the hearing. His mom had her head resting on Lester's shoulder and her eyes closed. At least she was safe. Lester would keep her safe. Ray knew Bryan would talk to them and offer encouraging words, just as he always offered them to Ray. Ray wanted to be excited, but he didn't have a lot of faith. He knew that his evidence was compelling, but it was being presented to the same old cast of characters who had put Ray away to begin with, plus the assistant attorney general who thought he was nothing but a waste of time. When he got back to his cell he ignored the questions of the guys asking how it went. Even the guards wanted to know and seemed hopeful that he might get released. Some nights, however, just called for silence and prayer. And on the row, there were a lot of bad days and a lot of bad nights, and if someone didn't want to talk, everyone knew to back off. Survival was at stake, and they cared enough for each other to let each other survive in their own way.

When Ray overheard a bootleg book discussion, the reminder of the days when they'd still had the club made him sad. All he could think of were those empty chairs in the library as they killed each of the prisoners off, one by one. First Larry, then Horsley; Henry, then Brian, and finally Victor. Nothing but empty chairs with every execution.

After they had officially closed down the book club, the books they had read, plus some new ones, circulated around the cells. There was no meeting in the library, but guys would talk about the books, yelling from cell to cell. If someone hadn't read the book, they just listened. If they had read the book, they could give ideas, offer opinions. And the questions always came to Ray, as if he was the book club teacher. He told the guys that he didn't have all the answers; there was no right or wrong in book club. You just had your own thoughts and interpretations and beliefs and ideas. That concept was new for a lot of guys. Giving their honest opinion, and having that listened to and respected was a new kind of drug that traveled around the row. Matters of the heart were discussed. Politics were discussed. Racism and poverty were discussed. Violence was discussed. Everyone had a chance to talk their way through the big ideas.

"Ray! You listening, Ray?" It was a guy named Jimmy Dill. Jimmy was a former drug addict who had been going to nursing school before he was convicted of robbing and killing a man for cocaine and a couple hundred bucks. Jimmy looked a bit unsure of himself when he talked; he loved to eat, and all day long he would talk about his favorite foods. Okra. Biscuits. Fried chicken. All day long. But Jimmy also had a kindness about him that made it hard to imagine him shooting someone in the back of the head.

"What you need, Jimmy?" Ray asked.

"I want to read that book *To Kill a Mockingbird*. Do you have it?"

"I have it."

"Can you send it my way with the guards next time they come round?" he asked.

"I can."

"Okay. Johnson wants to read it too; we're going to talk about it after. I've heard it's good. I don't know if that white boy is gonna understand it, but we'll see what he has to say."

Ray heard a few of the guys laugh. This was how it worked, and the book or books would get passed around, and then one day, without any planning, someone would yell, "How about that Scout girl?" and the discussion would begin.

That summer was hot and slow. Bryan and Ray were waiting for word back from Judge Garrett about his Rule 32 petition, but there was nothing but silence. Ray couldn't imagine it would take him more than the summer to rule. He was the judge in the original trial. Garrett knew the case inside and out. Ray used to pray that the truth would come out; now he was praying that the truth would be heard. The truth was proven in that hearing. Ray was innocent. He had been set up and thrown away. Now he needed Garrett to do the right thing, the honorable thing.

Lester came to visit in August on what had to be the hottest day of the year. It felt like it was 120 degrees in the shade, and without air, Ray thought they were all going to melt into a puddle on the visiting yard. He tried to keep his visiting whites clean and fresh, but he was sweating so hard that he decided to cut the visit short just so Lester and Sia could get back to the air-conditioning in the car.

"Lester, before you go, one more thing," Ray said.

"What's that? What do you need?" That was Lester. He got Ray everything he needed even before he needed it. Lester made sure he never went without commissary or a television and radio or extra socks and shorts.

"I need my birth certificate."

"Your what?"

"I'm going to need my birth certificate for when I get out of here. I won't have any identification. I'm going to need some, and all I'm going to have to prove I am who I am is my birth certificate."

Lester was quiet for a minute or so. He looked down at the ground and then took a breath. "You are going to need that," he said. And then he gave Ray a big smile. "How should I go about getting it? I will mail it to you, but tell me where to find it."

"You know God can do everything but fail, right?"

"That's right."

"Well, God is going to have to release me or be proven a liar."

"How do you figure that?"

"'What things soever you desire when you pray, believe that you receive them, and you shall have them.' Mark 11:24," Ray said.

Lester smiled. He knew this was Ray's favorite Scripture, and Ray had talked about it a million times before. "What about it?"

"God can't fail. Therefore, this Scripture has to be true, and I have to be set free or God is a liar because he would have failed."

"You're trying to trap God in some kind of loophole?" Lester laughed. "Man, you really should've been a lawyer."

"Maybe I will be. Maybe I will get out of here, go to law school, and start working with Bryan to start freeing all these innocent men up in here. Put an end to the death penalty once and for all. Maybe I will." Ray was forty-six years old, and he figured they both knew he was too old to go to law school even if he walked out of there with Bryan. They laughed, and talked about some of the different things Ray might do when he was free.

"Okay. I'll get you your birth certificate," Lester said. "I'll talk to your sister."

"Why don't you ask my mom? She might have it."

A shadow passed over Lester's face for a brief second. There was something there that Ray didn't want to look at or think about.

"Okay. I'll ask them both, and I'll get it."

Ray looked over at Sia, who was smiling as big as could be. "What are you smiling at?"

"You're going to walk out of here, Ray," she said. "We all know it. And it's going to be a happy day. A bright day. It's going to be soon. We'll get the birth certificate, and then you can come to our house and cook us some dinner."

"You'd better count on it," Ray said.

* * *

"Ray, I got some news for you."

It was September 22, 2002, when the captain of the guards came to Ray's cell and said those words.

Ray felt his heart begin to pound. This didn't look like news of his release. He had seen enough death in there to know the way it showed on a man's face. The guard had death on his face, and even before he said what he came to say, the screaming began in Ray's head.

"It's your mom, Ray. She died today. We just got word. I'm sorry. The other guards and I want to offer our condolences."

Ray didn't say a word. The screaming in his head was so loud he just wanted the man to leave so he could put the pillow over his ears. He turned his back to the guard and wondered if he was going to pass out. The guard cleared his throat, and then Ray heard his footsteps walk away.

Ray cried quietly at first. And then it was as if his body were possessed, because he started shaking so hard he couldn't even hold his hand in front of his face. Was he having a seizure? He didn't care. Ray felt his stomach turn over, and he ran to the toilet, thinking he might throw up. All he wanted was his mama, and she was dead. Ray couldn't understand what kind of world this was now. He was nothing. He was nobody. People called him Ray, but he was Buhlar Hinton's son, and Buhlar Hinton was dead.

Ray started sobbing, and it was like his body was turning itself inside out. She had died and Ray wasn't with her. He couldn't live with that. He couldn't even breathe with that thought. He was in prison, on death row, and he didn't get to hold his mom as she passed. He would never get to hold her again. He couldn't tell her he loved her. He couldn't tell her goodbye.

When are they going to let you come home, baby?

Soon, Mama. I'm going to be home soon.

He had lied to his mom. He hadn't come home. He had lied to her, and she had died without Ray to take care of her. None of it mattered anymore. Bryan. The hearing. Whether he lived or died. Getting out of prison. What did it matter? His mama was dead. He'd thought he was going home to her, but she had gone to her eternal home first. It felt like a million razors were slicing through his chest. Maybe he could have a heart attack. He could drop dead and be with her in moments.

I'll be home soon, Mama. I promise.

Ray didn't know how long he cried. When he lifted his head up, the lights were out. He knew word had gotten around the row, but he had ignored people trying to send him coffee and he had ignored their condolences. Ray just didn't care anymore. He wasn't going to recover from this one. He couldn't go somewhere in his mind and pretend his mother wasn't dead. He was a condemned man on death row who couldn't convince anyone he was innocent.

He lay on his back for hours, and then he heard a deep voice say, *The only person who believed you were innocent is gone.*

Ray nodded, and the voice continued.

Why keep fighting? Why let them execute you? Take away their power.

There's nothing to live for now. Let Bryan Stevenson save someone else.

There's no use in staying here. They are never going to let you leave.

No one cares if you live or die. They're going to kill you one way or another.

On and on the voice went, and Ray listened to it. He listened to it until it took him to the darkest place he had ever been in his life, darker even than those first three years on the row. His mother was always the flicker of light in those years, but now she was gone and there was nothing but darkness.

Flatness.

It was like all light ceased to exist. There was no hope. There was no love. His life was over, and Ray knew this in the quiet way you know some things to be true.

He had failed.

There was nothing left inside him to keep him going. He didn't want to live. He felt like he didn't deserve to live. He didn't have the strength to live. They had won, and Ray was okay with that. He was ready to go.

Ray took a deep breath. His face felt raw in the darkness. His eyes were swollen and gritty. He had to die. He just had to figure out how to do it.

"Boy, I didn't raise no quitter!"

Ray heard his mother's voice loud and sharp, and he automatically flinched because he knew that tone of voice always preceded a smack upside the head.

He sat up in his bed.

"I didn't raise a quitter, and you're not going to quit."

Ray looked around his cell in the darkness. He didn't believe in ghosts, but he could hear his mama's voice as plain as the day is long.

"You're going to get out of here. You're going to keep fighting."

"I'm tired, Mama; I want to be with you," Ray whispered. "I want to hurt them like they've hurt us. They want to kill me, and I don't want to give them that chance."

"There's a time to live and a time to die. This is my time to die. No use crying about it. You knew I had cancer. You didn't want to talk about it, but you knew."

Ray started crying again. She was right. He had known.

"This isn't your time to die, son. It's not. You have work to do. You have to prove to them that my baby is no killer. You have to show them. You are a beacon. You are the light. Don't you listen to that fool devil telling you to give up. I didn't raise no child of mine to give up when things get tough. Your life isn't your life to take. It belongs to God. You have work to do. Hard work. I'm going to talk at you all night long if I have to and all day and all night again, and I will never stop until you know who you are. You were not born to die in this cell. God has a purpose for you. He has a purpose for all of us. I've served his purpose."

Ray cried softly as he heard her voice.

"Now, you wipe them tears, Ray, and you get up and you get in service to someone else. There's no time to be crying about yourself. There's no cause to be listening to the devil's voice in your head telling you that nothing matters. It all matters. You matter. You are his baby, and you matter more than anything in the world. When I'm done talking at you, I'm going to be talking at God. He's going to listen to me, if I have to talk to him for all eternity. He's going to get you out of there, or he's going to have a hard time of it, that's for sure."

"Okay, Mama. Okay," Ray whispered.

"Don't disappoint me, Ray. I taught you to believe in yourself even if no one else in the world believes in you. Do you believe in you? Do you?"

Ray nodded in the darkness.

He was Anthony Ray Hinton. People called him Ray. He was Buhlar Hinton's son.

That's my baby.

"I'm going to talk to God, and we're going to give Mr. Bryan Stevenson a little help from here. There's a time to live and a time to die, Ray."

"Yes, Mama."

"And it will never be your time to die in that place. Never."

"Yes, Mama."

"I'm not fooling this time, Ray. Don't make me come back here."

They may beat you now and then, but that don't mean they can break you.

Ray fell asleep then, a deep, dreamless sleep, and when he woke up, it was long after breakfast, almost time for lunch.

The gifts started arriving immediately after he woke up. Coffee. Chocolate. Sweets of all kinds. Cards. Books. Death row was holding its own memorial in the only way it knew how.

"She loved you a lot, Ray. I've never seen a mother love her son more."

"She's proud of you."

"Rest in peace, Ray."

"I'm sorry, Ray."

"My condolences, Ray."

All through the day and into the night, men shouted out their words of sympathy. Sorrow shared was sorrow lessened.

And then Ray heard Jimmy Dill.

"Ray!" Jimmy yelled. "Can you help me with something?"

Ray took a deep breath. His mama had told him to be in service to someone else.

"What do you need?"

"In the book, it says, 'They've done it before and they did it tonight and they'll do it again and when they do it—seems that only children weep.' What does that mean, exactly?"

Ray smiled. It seemed book club had started. "Well, Atticus says that after the verdict, right?"

"Yeah."

"I think it's because only the child cries when an innocent man is convicted. All the adults just accept it. It's happened before, and it will happen again. What do you think?" Ray asked.

"I think that's right, Ray. I think that's right. But here's what I want to say. Just because they've done it before and they'll do it again doesn't mean you stop fighting, right? I don't think it's something people should ever get used to, do you?"

You need to choose who you are, Ray. You need to choose what sort of man you are going to be. You need to choose now. I know you will choose right. I know you will.

"I don't think people should get used to injustice," Ray said.

"You know what we have to do then, Ray, right? You know what we always have to do?"

"What's that?"

"You have to fight, Ray. You have to never stop fighting."

And if Ray didn't know better, he would have thought that the voice of his mother was coming out of a convicted killer on death row by the name of Jimmy Dill.

Chapter Twenty-Two

JUSTICE TOO LONG DELAYED IS JUSTICE DENIED

"It's really bad that it's gone on this long without a final resolve on it, and I'll take part of the responsibility for that."
—Judge James Garrett, January 28, 2002

Phoebe, Lester's mom, visited Ray after his mom died, and even though it wasn't supposed to be allowed, the guards looked the other way as she put her arms around him and held him as he cried all over her shoulder. Lester kept clearing his throat and wiping at his eyes. Ray's mom was also his mom, and he had taken care of her for almost twenty years. Ray had lost his mom, and Lester's mom had lost her best friend.

"I want you to know something, Ray," she said, patting him on the back like she used to do when he was a little boy. "One of us is always going to be here, until the very end. No matter what, one of us will always be here. Do you understand?"

Ray nodded and swallowed his tears. He was grateful to have them. How could he have survived this long without them?

"No matter what," she said again, and then she kissed him one last time on the top of his head.

When she passed away a couple of years later, Lester and Ray cried together and then had a good laugh about how God was really in trouble now. There was going to be no sleep or peace in heaven until those two women got their way and God set Ray free.

Still no word from Judge Garrett. Bryan wrote letter after letter, filed brief after brief, and still nothing. After a year, Bryan decided that pressure from the public might be the only way to get the State to do the right thing, and he began contacting the media about his story.

November 19, 2003

Anthony Ray Hinton, Z-468 Holman State Prison Holman, 3700 Atmore, Alabama 36503

Dear Ray:

How are you? I hope you're hanging in there. I wanted to update you on a couple of matters. Judge Garrett, as you know, has retired effective November 1. We heard that he would keep some cases and give others to different judges. While we can't get any definite indication, it appears as if he intends to keep your case. Following the debate I had with Pryor, I pressed him for what he was willing to do. He has indicated that they won't do anything but wait for Judge Garrett's ruling. While this is disappointing, it's not surprising.

Today, I've sent a letter to the chief deputy district attorney just so that we can represent to the press that these folks have had every opportunity to do the right thing. Our experts have similarly pressed the guy the State brought to your hearing from the Department of Forensic Sciences about doing something. No one appears to want to claim any responsibility, so we will have to put more pressure on them publicly.

I'm meeting with someone from the New York Times
*next week about an article, and I think we'll also work with
someone from a national magazine.* 60 Minutes *is supposed to
call Pryor this week. I'm worried about them because they keep
talking about the war with Iraq and are becoming somewhat
vague on when they'll actually do something. Anyway, I'm
supposed to talk with them again on Friday.*

*I'll be down to see you during the first week of
December because we will likely need to facilitate some
interviews between you and the* Times *reporter and the
magazine reporter next month. I want to talk to you some about
that before it begins. Things have been typically busy here, but
we're pressing on. I look forward to seeing you, my friend.*

Sincerely,
Bryan A. Stevenson

Another nine months passed, and they still had no answer
on his Rule 32 hearing. Bryan was frustrated, and Ray couldn't
imagine how Bryan managed, with so many lives depending
on him. Ray kept telling him that if things didn't turn out the
way they wanted, he knew Bryan had done everything he could.
Eventually, Bryan went straight to the source.

September 23, 2004

Judge James Garrett
c/o Anne-Marie Adams, Clerk Jefferson County Circuit Court
207 Criminal Justice Center
801 N. Richard Arrington, Jr. Blvd. Birmingham, AL 35203

Dear Judge Garrett:

I'm writing to inquire about the status of the Anthony Ray Hinton case. As you know, Mr. Hinton is on Alabama's death row, although we maintain and have presented evidence that he is innocent and had nothing to do with these crimes. Over two years ago, we presented evidence in support of Mr. Hinton's claim of factual innocence. I know that since that time you have retired, which is why I'm writing to determine the status of this case and whether you are still reviewing the case. We filed a renewed motion for a judgment granting relief on February 23, 2004, and we have not been able to confirm from the clerk's office whether you received that pleading or our subsequent requests for a ruling.

While I appreciate that the length of time required in death penalty cases has been an issue for lots of people, we're especially concerned about this case because we believe that the evidence clearly supports Mr. Hinton's innocence and that he has now been wrongly held on Alabama's death row for nineteen years.

I would greatly appreciate it if you could inform the parties of the case status or determine what, if any, other arrangements have been made for a resolution of this case. I'm sorry to disturb you with a letter of this sort, but I genuinely believe that Mr. Hinton is innocent and this case represents a terrible mistake.

I appreciate your consideration of this matter and sincerely hope that all is well with you.

Respectfully, Bryan A. Stevenson
Counsel for Anthony Ray Hinton
cc: James Houts, Assistant Attorney General Jon Hayden,
Assistant Attorney General
J. Scott Vowell, Presiding Judge

Bryan sent Ray a letter at the end of January explaining that Judge Garrett had done absolutely nothing for two and a half years, then just signed the State's proposed order. Ray read it aloud to the other guys. A couple of the guards stood in the hallway listening as well.

> *While it's not surprising, it builds another layer into the worst example of corrupt, unjust administration of the death penalty anywhere. We knew not to expect much from him in terms of relief, but he didn't have to unnecessarily take another two and a half years of your life for no good reason.*
>
> *Garrett printed out the State's order and changed the margins; I guess he thought that made it look better. But it appears word for word to be the State's proposed order. I attach it even though I think we sent you the State's order a couple of years ago. You may recall that we filed a lengthy response challenging the State's proposed order, which I'm also resending in case you don't have that anymore.*

Bryan promised to forge ahead, and ended as usual, with support and encouragement.

> *We've called your family and Lester Bailey, and I'm sending stuff to our experts today, who I expect to be pretty*

outraged about this too. I'll look to talk with you on Monday
afternoon.

Hang in there.

Sincerely,
Bryan
P.S. Jerline got the package you sent and absolutely loves it!
Thank you for doing that.

There it was, the ugly truth. The State would lie, cheat, steal, and stall to keep from admitting they were wrong about Ray. Evidence didn't matter. Nothing seemed to matter. Bryan was furious and filed an appeal with the Alabama Court of Criminal Appeals. A hearing was scheduled, and Bryan had upped the ante involving Amnesty International, the local news, and the national news.

In August, George Sibley was executed. His last words were, "Everyone who is doing this to me is guilty of a murder." Ray banged on the bars for him and said a prayer for George's son. He wondered what it was like for that boy to have both his parents executed. It was too much for any person to carry.

> • As of June 11, 2020, capital punishment is legal in twenty-eight U.S. states. In 2021, Governor Ralph Northam abolished the death penalty in Virginia, making it the first Southern state to do so.[24]

---

24 https://deathpenaltyinfo.org/state-and-federal-info/state-by-state/virginia

- Since 1976, when the death penalty was reinstated by the U.S. Supreme Court, states have executed 1,516 people (as of July 2020).[25]

- Since 1973, there have been 170 death row exonerations (as of July 2020). Twenty-nine of them are from the state of Florida.[26]

- A Death Penalty Information Center (DPIC) study of thirty years of FBI Uniform Crime Report homicide data found that the South has consistently had by far the highest murder rate. The South accounts for more than 80 percent of executions. The Northeast, which has fewer than 0.5 percent of all executions, has consistently had the lowest murder rate.

In November 2005, a series of articles ran in the *Birmingham News*. Ray did an interview by telephone. The series of articles was about the death penalty, for and against. Bryan wrote the piece against, and as Ray read the article to the other guys on the row, he was proud to call Bryan not only his attorney, but his friend.

Ray read the article again and again. Next to it in the paper was an opposing opinion piece—pro death penalty—by the attorney general, Troy King. His basic argument was an eye for an eye, and Ray understood that. He had grown up with that in church. Justice demanded a life for a life. Retribution.

25 www.cnn.com/2013/07/19/us/death-penalty-fast-facts
26 Ibid.

The perpetrator should not live while the victim has no choice. People on death row had earned their spots on death row, and justice cannot be consumed with protecting the rights of the guilty. But the system didn't know who was guilty. There was a moral difference between kidnapping and murdering a man, and imprisoning and executing a man. There was no moral equivalence, even when both things ended in death. But death had never deterred death. And guilt could not be certain without an admission of guilt. A person could believe in the death penalty and still believe it should be ended, because men are fallible and the justice system is fallible.

Ray believed that until the U.S. had a way of ensuring that innocent men are never executed—until the nation could account for the racism in its courts, prisons, and in its sentencing—the death penalty should be abolished. Let Troy King spend a decade or two in prison under a sentence of death as an innocent man and see what kind of opinion he writes then.

There was no humane way to execute any man.

And regardless of any law, no one had the right to execute an innocent man. One line in particular in the pro article struck him: "To be sure, the death sentence must never be carried out in a way that allows the innocent to die." There was an irony there. If he believed that, why was he refusing to objectively look at the evidence of Ray's innocence?

Bryan's editorial was moving and impressive. Even the guards were reading pieces of it out loud. Ray didn't know what was going to happen in appeals court, but he did know that he still had God's best lawyer fighting for him.

On the day of the hearing, another article came out quoting

both Ray and McGregor. He was still mad twenty years later that Ray had stared him down in the courtroom, and he also threatened that if Ray was released, he'd be "standing right outside the gate with a .38 and it won't be an old one." Ray hoped that quote would help prove his case to the appeals court. Two decades later and he was still saying, on the record, he was going to get Ray one way or another. Bryan seemed hopeful after the oral arguments.

November 30, 2005

Anthony Ray Hinton, Z-468 Holman State Prison Holman,
3700
Atmore, Alabama 36503

Dear Ray:

How are you, my friend? Last week, the State filed another pleading in your case following oral argument. It's amazing that they now want to discuss the evidence in your case after saying for so many years everything is barred and defaulted. In any event, they have filed a motion to supplement their brief because I stressed the fact that the gun evidence exonerates you so much at oral argument, I think they are worried about that. I attach a copy of what they sent. We filed a response to their pleading yesterday, which is also enclosed with this letter. I think it's good that they now feel some need to address the merits of these issues. The letters to the newspaper following the Birmingham News *articles have all been good.*

I'll get copies of them to you as soon as we have them collected.

I'm really hoping that you've had your last Thanksgiving on death row. It's always better to not get too optimistic when you are dealing with the Alabama justice system, but you deserve relief soon.

I'm going to try and get down before Christmas. The court issued a bunch of decisions in older cases last week, so we've been pretty busy. I hope you're doing okay. All the best, my friend.

Sincerely,
Bryan Stevenson

Ray tried not to get too hopeful as they were waiting for the Court of Criminal Appeals. He kept as busy as possible and was grateful the guards let him spend much of the day in their break room. He would cook for them and counsel them on everything from money problems to marriage issues. It was pretty ironic that they came to Ray for advice when he had spent over two decades locked in a cell and cut off from the outside world. He also helped deliver meals to the guys on the row. It was a way to say hi to each of them, to look in their eyes and see if he saw signs that they were heading to the dark place they all knew too well.

He was doing what his mom wanted, he was in service to others. It got him through each day of each month until his visit with Lester.

At the end of June 2006, Ray got the news from Bryan: the Alabama Court of Criminal Appeals had denied his appeal. They were now going to appeal to the Alabama Supreme Court. Ray went back to his cell and told the other guys. Jimmy seemed especially upset. Ray's freedom was a cause that everyone on the row wanted to fight for. The newspaper articles had established his innocence in a way that was more real than anything he'd said over the years. No one doubted his innocence, and after Bryan's article, Ray had told them all that when he got out, he was going to fight to end the death penalty. Ray had dreams where he spoke at colleges, in churches, around the country, and across the globe. He was going to tell his story so that this never happened to anyone else.

But first he had to be set free.

So in 2006, they were going to another court, one that Ray had appealed to back in 1989. It was like his case was bouncing around inside a State pinball machine. Circuit Court. Appeals Court. Supreme Court and back again. Over and over. Ray wasn't upset, though—on the contrary, he was ecstatic. The ruling in the Alabama Court of Criminal Appeals was 3–2. It was a ruling against him, but for the first time, two judges believed in his innocence.

Dissent was a beautiful thing. And it was all he had.

Chapter Twenty-Three

THEY KILL YOU ON THURSDAYS

"The scale and the brutality of our prisons are the moral scandal of American life."

—Adam Gopnik[27]

Bryan and Ray appealed to the Alabama Supreme Court, and the court refused to rule until a determination was made as to whether Payne was a qualified expert. So, back down the ladder. Judge Garrett was gone—completely retired—and had let go of Ray's case. Ray was hopeful that the new circuit court judge—Laura Petro—might be a bit more receptive to his case.

It took until March 2009 before Judge Petro ruled.

March 11, 2009

Anthony Ray Hinton, Z-468 Holman State Prison Holman, 3700
Atmore, Alabama 36503

Dear Ray:

Well, unfortunately, Judge Petro did not help us. She wrote a very bizarre order which attempts to only address what she

---

*thinks Judge Garrett thought of Payne. She concludes that
she thinks that Judge Garrett thought Payne was competent.
We'll interpret this as Petro being unwilling to independently
find Payne competent. Very disappointing. Call me. I'll be
around all next week if you want to talk and we can discuss
next steps. Because this order is so bizarre, it's a better order
than if she did what the court actually ordered which is
to make independent findings about Payne's competence.
Anyway, I said I'd write unless there was good news so I
wanted to get this in the mail to you right away. I'll speak
with you soon.*

Hang in there.

Sincerely, Bryan Stevenson

It was getting harder for Ray to hang in there. Jimmy Dill
was scheduled to be executed in a month. Since the day
Ray had hoped he would spend his last Thanksgiving on the
row, he had watched thirty-seven men be put to death. In 2009,
two had already been put to death that year. Ray had watched
ten men die since Garrett had denied his Rule 32 petition. The
mood on the row was solemn. There were no more bootleg
book club discussions. They were all just trying to survive, and
the younger guys who came in were angry and agitated in a way
Ray had never seen before. They had no interest in discussing
literature. And it only became tenser between the guards and
the men on the row when an execution date was set. Because
execution was now by lethal injection, they didn't practice turning on the generator anymore, but they still practiced their routines for putting someone to death.

"We'd never kill you, Ray," one guard used to say. "I'm just doing my job."

"You volunteer for this, man. You volunteer to be on the Death Squad. I know it. You know it. All the guys know it."

"I'm just doing my job."

Ray knew that the guards would kill him if he got an execution date. They knew it too. There would be no way around it. What would happen if they all just refused to kill? If they took a stand? How could they take the inmates to the doctor, feed them, commiserate with them, and then lead them to their deaths? It messed with the prisoners' minds after a while. The guards were their family also. They were all in this dark, dank, tiny corner of the world acting out some perverse play where they laughed together six days of the week, but on Thursdays, these same guards killed the men on the row.

Ray's case went back to the Court of Criminal Appeals, and they bounced it back down to Judge Petro again because, as Bryan had said, she didn't rule on whether Payne was a qualified expert, only on what she thought Garrett had believed in 1986.

In September 2010, Judge Petro ruled that Payne was an expert because he "had acquired a knowledge of firearms identification beyond that of an ordinary witness." Ray thought that was like the court saying he was qualified as a heart surgeon because he'd once had an EKG. In other words, complete nonsense. So, Bryan and Ray bounced back up to the appeals court, which affirmed the lower court, and sent them back up to the Alabama Supreme Court. Aaaand . . . they punted his case back down, saying the wrong standard had been applied when the court determined Payne was a qualified expert.

It was enough to make a man dizzy.

Bryan never gave up, and Ray could see how hard this was on him. He carried the world on his shoulders, and there were visits where Ray could see the strain and the stress in his eyes. Ray wasn't his only case, and neither of them were getting any younger. Ray was tired, and he had stopped praying for the truth to be known. The truth *was* known. Alabama knew he was innocent, but they would never admit it.

They wouldn't in 1986.

They wouldn't in 2002.

They wouldn't in 2005.

And they weren't going to in 2013.

Bryan had an arrangement that he would get a message to the prison when he needed to talk to Ray. Because there had been so much press when there were rulings on his case, they ended up on the local news. Court rulings came in around 2:00 p.m. The news ran at 5:00 p.m. Bryan didn't ever want Ray to find out about his case on the news first.

When Ray got the message to call Bryan, he tried to keep his expectations low.

"They denied us, Ray. I'm sorry."

Ray held the phone away from his ear. He had been so sure that there would be a miracle. He had been so certain that because two judges had finally taken his side, everything would be fixed.

He was never going to get out of there.

He was going to be slowly and painfully killed by a toxic drug cocktail from the inside out. He was going to be put to sleep like a stray, rabid dog. That was how much his life mattered—maybe even less. The dog would have comfort in his death, perhaps.

Ray would miss this life. He would miss Bryan. He knew Bryan had watched men he cared about die. Ray had too. There are no words for the scars that leaves. There are no words for how every death kills a little piece of your humanity. Your soul dies a little, your mind cracks a bit, your heart pounds and bleeds as a piece of it tears off. A mind, and a heart, and a soul could only take so much.

Ray wiped at his tears and took a deep breath before he held the phone back up to his ear. Bryan was still talking. "Maybe I didn't do enough. I should have—"

Ray's heart ached for this man, so he interrupted him. "Mr. Stevenson, this is Ray Hinton's assistant, and he asked me to tell you to go on home now; it's Friday. He said you have yourself a nice dinner, drink a glass of wine, watch a movie . . . do whatever it takes to feel better, and he said that you should just forget about Ray Hinton for the weekend."

"Ray—" Bryan tried to interrupt.

"This is Ray Hinton's assistant, and he said to tell you that if they let him go outside this weekend, he is going to shoot some basketball and relax and take some time away from all these legal matters. He said you should do the same, and he'll call you first thing Monday morning."

Bryan laughed softly.

"Ray also said you have his permission to enjoy your entire weekend. Enjoy the sunshine. Take a nice walk in the woods. Forget about Ray Hinton, because Ray Hinton is going to forget about Ray Hinton for a while."

"You tell him thank you for me." Ray could hear that Bryan's voice was lighter.

"You can tell him yourself when he calls you Monday

morning." Then Ray hung up the phone and went back to his cell. What lawyer needs a convict's permission to go out and enjoy his weekend? Bryan cared about him so much that it moved Ray in a way that was beyond words. He knew Bryan was doing everything he could to save his life. Bryan deserved to have a weekend free of the burden. Ray wanted Bryan to hold his face up toward the sunshine. To experience some much-deserved moments away from the horrors of the prisons, away from the disappointment of the courts.

It was dark in Ray's cell, darker than it should have been for 5:00 p.m. in April. He wondered if he would ever get a chance to turn his face to the sun as a free man. He wondered if there would come a time when the fight was over.

On Monday morning at 9:00 sharp, Ray yelled to the guards that he needed the telephone, and he called Bryan's office collect.

"Ray, how are you doing this morning?" Bryan asked.

"I'm fine, Bryan. How was your weekend?"

"I had a great weekend, Ray, a really great weekend." Ray could tell by his voice that it was true.

But the weekend was over.

"Well, it's 9:00 a.m., and I told you I would call, so now get back to work on my case!"

Bryan laughed. "I'm going to come see you. I have something I'd like to talk to you about in person."

"You have an idea about what to do next?"

"I do, Ray. I do."

They said their goodbyes, and Ray was happy to know that Bryan wasn't giving up yet. If he wasn't giving up, then Ray wasn't going to give up either.

Ray gave Lester the news the next time he visited.

As promised, Lester had gotten Ray's birth certificate, and they talked a little bit about where Ray would go if he ever got out. His mom's house had been empty for ten years and would need a lot of repairs before it was habitable again.

They had been talking about Ray walking out of prison for twenty-seven years.

Before long, he would be on death row for longer than he had been a free man. Ray and Lester were putting less into their dreams about the future. They were both getting old. Ray looked at Lester, and for a second, his whole time on death row flashed before his eyes—but this time without Lester in it. Lester, his friend, his brother, had never missed a visit since he had been arrested in 1985. It was 2013. The world had changed, but Lester's friendship had remained the same. Tears formed in Ray's eyes.

"What's wrong?" asked Lester.

"Remember those days when we used to walk home and jump in the ditch and hide?" Ray asked.

"Yeah, I remember."

"What were we afraid of, exactly?"

Lester didn't say anything. He just stared at Ray, and his eyes were sadder than Ray had ever seen them before.

"I'm getting tired," Ray said. "The court denied my rehearing. I don't think I have many more options. They don't seem to care about the new evidence. They don't seem in any hurry. They're going to either give me a date or bounce me around from court to court until I die. For the first time in a long time, I don't know if I'm going to walk out of here. I just don't know."

"You can't stop fighting."

"Why? Why can't I stop fighting?" Ray wasn't being funny. He was just so tired. "I've lived a full life."

Lester gave a grunt like he didn't believe him.

"Lester, I've won Wimbledon five times. I've played third base for the Yankees and led the league in home runs for ten straight years. I've traveled the world. I've married the most beautiful women. I've loved and I've laughed and I've lost God and found God again and wondered for too many hours what the purpose is for me going to death row for something I didn't do. And sometimes I think there is no purpose—that this is just the life I was meant to live. I've made a home here and a family out of some of the most terrifying men you'd ever meet. And you know what I've learned? We're all the same. We're all guilty of something, and we're all innocent at the same time. And I'm sorry, but a man can go crazy trying to make it all fit into some plan. Maybe this is the plan. Maybe I was born to live most of my life in a five-by-seven so I could travel the world. I would have never won Wimbledon if I hadn't gone to death row. Do you see what I'm saying, Lester? Do you understand what I'm saying?"

Lester cleared his throat. "I remember walking home with you and jumping in that ditch and you saying to me that it's strange what a person could get used to. Do you remember that?"

Ray shook his head. He didn't remember that.

"Well, you said it. And you know why we were so afraid? Do you know why, Ray?"

"No. Why?"

"We were afraid because we couldn't see what was coming at

us. So we hid in those ditches. We hid rather than face whatever might be in front of us."

Ray nodded.

"We're not kids anymore, Ray, and we're not afraid. We're not going to hide in a ditch together. We're going to face whatever happens. We're going to face it, and we're going to fight if we have to fight, and we're not going to ever get used to this. You were not born to die on death row. I know that for a fact."

Lester had never been a talker, but he had something to say this time.

"Okay," Ray said.

Ray didn't ever want to get used to this.

He didn't want this to ever be normal.

There was beauty if he looked for it.

He had his best friend at his side.

"We're still walking home, Ray. We're still just walking home together."

When Ray walked into the visiting area and saw Bryan waiting, Bryan's expression was serious. More than serious, he looked determined in a way Ray hadn't seen before. They'd had so many denials, so many phone calls where Bryan had to tell Ray they'd ruled against him again, that sometimes they didn't even want to talk about his case. Sometimes they just laughed. At nothing in particular, and everything. Some days they were like two teenagers who can't stop laughing even when their teacher yells at them. Some days it all seemed so bizarre that Ray was still in that prison that they just had to laugh their heads off. It felt good to laugh like that. Ray felt like it kept them young, and it kept them sane.

Bryan smiled when Ray walked up. "How you doing, my friend?"

"I'm doing all right."

"Listen, I have an idea. I want you to really think about everything I'm about to say before you decide. We've got some strategic decisions to make."

Bryan explained that they could appeal through the lower state and federal courts, arguing things like suppression of evidence and ineffective counsel but they couldn't argue his innocence. "There's only one last opportunity for us to talk about your innocence, and that is if we go to the U.S. Supreme Court now. We can't claim innocence in the federal habeas, only how your federal rights were violated. The Supreme Court is not going to grant relief on the innocence claim alone, but I think we can present to them a narrative that might motivate them to do something. Your innocence will matter, Ray. It's the last time it will matter to a court."

Ray nodded again. He wanted his innocence to matter. He wanted it to matter forever.

"Listen, though. If they deny the cert, then nobody's going to ever listen to your innocence claim again. If we don't go to the Supreme Court now, we'll have another chance at the end of this federal habeas process, which could take years. You should know that. Be prepared for that. But when the Supreme Court reviews, then, it will be only a review on the very restricted issues we bring in federal habeas. What I mean is, they're not going to look at your innocence. They're going to be very narrow in what they consider, and the chance for relief will be greatly reduced."

"And in federal habeas, I can get bounced through different

courts again? Bounced back and forth, but just federal courts this time?"

"Pretty much," answered Bryan. "You know how the State's been with your appeal. That's not going to change. If anything, they're going to ramp up the opposition in federal habeas. I mean, we can go to the Supreme Court after for review, but we could be in litigation for years, and they rarely, I mean, it's going to be hard either way . . . and there's something else, Ray. If we take your case to the Supreme Court and we lose, things could speed up. It could make it harder for us to win in federal habeas and harder for us to stop them from killing you."

So basically, they could take their chances, and if the Supreme Court took the case and they won—Ray could be on the fast track to freedom. But if they did, and he lost . . . his execution date could come up sooner rather than later. If they didn't try for the Supreme Court now, they could spend years and years dealing with shenanigans and inertia in the lower federal courts.

Ray interrupted Bryan. "Do you have money for the vending machine? I'd like a drink."

"Sure, Ray. Sure." Bryan gave him some quarters, and Ray walked over and got a Coke out of the machine.

Ray sat back down and opened the soda. "A man needs a drink when he's making a big decision."

"Ray—"

Ray held up his hand to silence Bryan and drank a long swig of the soda. For the first time in his life, he wished he had some hard liquor. Ray had never been a drinker, but now he imagined that soda was full of scotch.

"Bryan, I'm innocent. I want the courts to admit I'm innocent. I want the world to know I'm innocent. I don't want life without parole. I want to walk out of here. I want to live the rest of my life a free man. I would rather die. If I can't prove my innocence, I would rather die."

"So what do you want to do, Ray? It could take another eight or nine months to file, and there's no guarantee and—"

"I want to go to the Supreme Court now, Bryan. I want them to know I'm innocent. I want them to hear my case now, when we can present everything. I don't want to spend another ten years in the courts. I don't think I can do it. I don't think I can be here until I'm seventy years old and still be fighting."

They were quiet for a while after that. Ray looked around the visiting area. He had spent so much time there over the last few decades. He had eaten a lot of key lime pie out of the vending machine. And he had come to respect and love this man who sat in front of him. He knew Bryan was tired too, and Ray was just one of many battles he was fighting. They both deserved a win.

It was time.

And if it wasn't, then Ray would take his Thursday. He would eat his last meal, and he would thank Lester for being the best friend a guy could ever have, and he would tell Bryan Stevenson that he couldn't save everyone. He'd tell Bryan that he knew he had done everything he could. He would have joy knowing that he lived as big a life as anyone ever could live in a five-by-seven cell.

And God have mercy on their souls, but Ray knew what his last words would be.

I am innocent.

Chapter Twenty-Four

JUSTICE FOR ALL

"As there is no issue here worthy of certiorari, this court should deny review in this matter."
—Luther Strange, Alabama attorney general, to the Supreme Court of the United States, November 2013

There are certain moments that stay with you. For a lot of people, it's when they get married or give birth to their first child. For others, it's when they get their first job, or meet the woman or man of their dreams, or maybe it's something as simple as being acknowledged by someone or finally getting the nerve to do something they've always been afraid of. Ray spent the six months it took for Bryan to file his petition with the U.S. Supreme Court reflecting on his moments—but only the good ones. He didn't want to review the bad moments. His mother's death. The arrest and conviction. The fifty-four human beings he had watched walk to their own executions. Ray knew all their names, and in July, the night before Andrew Lackey, a white man who had only been on the row for about five years, was taken to the death chamber, Ray said the names of fifty-three of them in his head. Some people count sheep. Ray counted the dead.

Wayne. Michael. Horace. Herbert. Arthur. Wallace. Larry. Neal. Willie. Varnall. Edward. Billy. Walter. Henry. Steven. Brian.

Victor. David. Freddie. Robert. Pernell. Lynda. Anthony. Michael. Gary. Tommy. JB. David. Mario. Jerry. George. John. Larry. Aaron. Darrell. Luther. James. Danny. Jimmy. Willie. Jack. Max. Thomas. John. Michael. Holly. Philip. Leroy. William. Jason. Eddie. Derrick. Christopher.

He didn't want to add Andrew's name to the list. Not yet. Not when there was still hope. The man before Andrew had only been there four years. Like Andrew, Christopher didn't want to appeal. They were young guys, but both seemed like they didn't know what was happening to them. Ray wasn't sure they really understood where they were or that they were choosing not to appeal their convictions. It was sad, and Ray felt older than his fifty-seven years. He banged on the bars for Christopher and for Andrew, just so they would know they weren't alone.

Ray had made noise for a lot of men as they faced their own deaths.

He tried to keep his mind focused on the good moments. The moments before his arrest were warm summer nights playing baseball with Lester and the other kids in Praco. They were so blissfully unaware of how dangerous the world was. Even the bombings and protests in Birmingham had seemed far away from their sanctuary in Praco. Ray wished they had never left there. *What if we had stayed in Praco and I had stayed in the mines? How would my life have turned out? What would have been my important moments?* What if he had married his Sylvia when he had the chance? *I would be a father, maybe even a grandfather by now. How many baseball games had I missed? How many walks in the woods? How many sunrises and sunsets could one man miss in his life and still have a life?* Ray had lived in darkness for so long, he almost couldn't imagine what it would be like to be a free man under a shining sun. He thought about what it felt like to make a woman laugh. Would he ever kiss a woman again? Even if he got out, who would want to kiss the man from death row? Ray tried to remember the moments he spent fishing with his mama or sitting next to her in church and praying. He remembered the food she used to make and the love that he could taste in every bite.

The good moments after coming to death row were harder. Doubled up laughing with Lester and Sylvia at visits. Telling them stories that kept them grinning and helped them to believe that life on death row wasn't as bad as it seemed. Sitting with Bryan talking about his case and also talking about football. Making him laugh. Seeing the strain leave his eyes for a half hour. Helping another man get through a long, dark night on the row. Just voices in the darkness calling out to each other. They all did their time differently. Ray traveled in his mind. Some guys never spoke. Some guys never stopped being angry. Some guys prayed to God, and some nurtured a darkness that Ray believed no man should ever carry. He tried to remember the moments on the row that would make his mama proud. He tried to focus on the moments that held light and laughter. It helped him get through. His case was winding down—he knew that. There was a clock counting down to the day he ran out of time—the day when he would get his execution date and would have to learn how to live with knowing the date and time of his death. Ray didn't want to know. He would rather it be a surprise than have to live out thirty or sixty days seeing the faces of the men practicing for his death.

It was hard not to spend time wishing for a different life, but Ray tried not to dwell on all the what-ifs. *What if I had never driven off in that car? What if I had taken a job somewhere besides Bruno's?*

What if I hadn't been born poor?

What if he'd had Bryan as his lawyer from the start? Ray was still fighting for his freedom, but it was with a quiet acceptance of what seemed inevitable. They were never going to admit they had put the wrong man on death row. Anthony Ray Hinton was never going to walk out of prison.

Bryan filed the petition for a writ of certiorari in the U.S. Supreme Court in October 2013, and the State filed their response in November. Bryan filed a response to their response a week after. There was no New Year's celebration on death row, and 2014 came in like a quiet thief in the night.

What could they celebrate, really—another year of being alive or another year of being closer to death?

How did free men celebrate a new year? Ray didn't know, and he couldn't remember.

It was near the end of February when Ray got word to call Bryan. Again. How many of those phone calls had he made over the last fifteen years? And how many had ever been good news?

Bryan seemed breathless when he got on the line. And excited. Ray tried not to get his hopes up, but he felt his heart start to beat faster.

"Ray, I only have a few moments, but I need to tell you—"

"What is it, Bryan? Did Kim Kardashian call looking for me?"

(Ray's imagination had brought him to a divorce from Sandra Bullock for Kim. It was all very dramatic—in his head.)

Bryan laughed. "No, Ray. The U.S. Supreme Court ruled."

Ray took in a breath. He hoped they were going to allow oral arguments. He knew Bryan could work his magic if he got in front of them. It was rare, Ray knew, but he had imagined it in his mind. Bryan pleading his innocence in front of the justices of the Supreme Court. Maybe even Obama. He could imagine the impossible. The country had a Black president, and nobody ever thought that would happen.

"Ray, it was a unanimous decision. They ruled on your case. They didn't say they would review; *they reviewed and ruled.* Here, let me read something to you."

"What do you mean, Bryan?" Ray asked. He couldn't understand what Bryan was saying.

"Listen to this: Anthony Ray Hinton, an inmate on Alabama's death row, asks us to decide whether the Alabama courts correctly applied Strickland to his case. We conclude that they did not and hold that Hinton's trial attorney rendered constitutionally deficient performance. We vacate the lower court's judgment and remand the case for reconsideration of whether the attorney's deficient performance was prejudicial."

Ray didn't say a word. Did he really understand what Bryan was saying?

Bryan went on, "The petition for certiorari and Hinton's motion for leave to proceed in forma pauperis are granted, the judgment of the Court of Criminal Appeals of Alabama is vacated, and the case is remanded for further proceedings not inconsistent with this opinion. It is so ordered."

"It is so ordered?"

"Ray, it is so ordered. By the United States Supreme Court. They didn't grant review; they ruled outright. In your favor. They overruled the appeals court. Ray, it was a unanimous decision."

Ray dropped the phone and sat down on the floor and wept

like a baby. Nine Supreme Court justices. Even the staunchly conservative Scalia, who believed that the death penalty was constitutional but affirmative action wasn't. They all believed him. Who was going to argue with them? Could Alabama?

It was a few moments before Ray picked up the phone and put it back to his ear. He didn't know if Bryan was still there.

"Bryan?"

"I'm here, Ray."

"Will you call Lester for me?"

"I will. Ray, we still have work ahead of us, and we have to go back through the state courts, but this is a win, Ray. A big win. They're going to have to issue you a new trial."

"When should I start packing?"

"Not yet, but hopefully soon. It's still going to take some time, and you still need to hang in there, but hopefully soon, my friend. Hopefully soon."

Ray went back to his cell, but he didn't tell anyone the news. He still had a ways to go, but for the first time in twenty-nine years, there was a flicker of light at the end of the tunnel. He didn't know how the appeals court was going to act now that the U.S. Supreme Court told them they had made an error. Because Perhacs hadn't asked for more money to hire a better expert, Ray's case had been devastated. Payne had been a horrible expert. Perhacs hadn't tried. The United States Supreme Court was on his side.

Ray couldn't believe it. All nine justices. Even Scalia.

The Court of Criminal Appeals sent Ray back down to circuit court—back to Judge Petro—so that court could determine whether Perhacs would have hired a better expert if he had known there was money to do so, and whether that expert would have led to reasonable doubt about his guilt. The answer was yes. On September 24, 2014, the circuit court found that Ray's trial was prejudiced—Perhacs's incompetence had done severe damage to his case. Perhacs was ineffective, and Ray's Rule 32 petition was granted. In December, Ray's case was going back to where it all started, in Jefferson County. Ray stayed awake in his cell and rang in the new year alone but with joy—2015. It was his only New Year's celebration in thirty years on death row. He wasn't free yet, but he was going to have a new trial, with Bryan Stevenson as his attorney and three of the best ballistics experts in the country testifying on his behalf. In January, the judge ordered Holman to have him back in Jefferson County for a February 18 hearing at 9:00 a.m.

Anthony Ray Hinton was finally leaving death row.

Not on a gurney. Not in a body bag.

Ray gave away his television and his tennis shoes. He passed out his commissary food and his books and his extra clothes. It was a joyful time on his block of the row. When the guard came to walk him out, he yelled out to the twenty-eight guys on his tier.

"Can I have your attention for a minute?" There were some hoots and hollers.

"I want you to know that I'm fixing to go. I'm leaving here. It took me thirty years to get to this moment. It may take thirty-one years for you. It may take thirty-two or thirty-three or thirty-five years, but you need to hold on. You need to hold on to your hope. If you have hope, you have everything."

The guys began to make a noise. They didn't bang on the bars like they usually did for executions; it was a joyful noise. It was a mixture of applause and laughter and chanting. "Hin-ton!

Hin-ton! Hin-ton!" Ray was taken back to high school and the basketball court and the time when he thought the crowd was chanting his name but they weren't. This time, they were and it was a strange mix of tragedy and sorrow and triumph and joy.

Ray walked off the row with his head held high and his birth certificate in his hand.

Free at last. Free at last.

Thank God Almighty, I'm free at last.

When he climbed into the van, he could see the cages he had walked in almost thirty years earlier. he could see the razor-wire fences and the dry, dusty yard. He never wanted to see this place again. He wasn't home yet, but he was one step closer.

Chapter Twenty-Five

THE SUN DOES SHINE

"You can't threaten to kill someone every day year after year and not harm them, not traumatize them, not break them in ways that are really profound."

—Bryan Stevenson

"They stole my 30s, they stole my 40s, they stole my 50s. I could not afford to give them my soul. I couldn't give them me."

—Anthony Ray Hinton[28]

Ray had just finished a meeting with one of Bryan's staff attorneys when the attorney came running back.

"Ray, Ray, you have to call Bryan. You have to call him as soon as you get back to the phones."

Ray wondered what it could be this time. He had been back in county jail for two months awaiting his new trial. A date hadn't been set yet. They had a few hearings, but things had gotten delayed because the district attorney's office couldn't find the gun or the bullets. They had actually accused Bryan of *stealing* them. It was incredible. *Bryan Stevenson* had supposedly stolen the most important evidence in his case. Bryan had to pull the transcripts from the 2002 hearing with Judge Garrett

---

28 www.themarshallproject.org/2015/04/09/30-years-on-death-row-a
-conversation-with-anthony-ray-hinton

to prove they had been admitted back into evidence then after being tested by his experts.

Later, the clerk found a box in a court storage facility off-site that had a bag in it with the gun and the bullets from his case. Lester said he was worried they were going to frame Ray again and send him back to the row, but Ray wasn't too worried. He had faith in Bryan. He had faith in the truth.

Ray got back to his cell block and went over to the bank of phones on the wall. He called Bryan's phone collect.

A young guy came up next to him. "What's going on, Pops?"

Ray pointed to the phone and shook his head at the kid. The guy was supposedly a big gang member. To Ray, he was one of the little wannabe gangsters there, playing at a game they knew nothing about. Ray wanted to sit each one of them down and show them their future if they didn't choose a better way. Life was precious. Their freedom was precious. They each had the potential to be so much more than whatever had landed them in jail. Ray didn't want any of them to end up on death row. He tried to tell them what it was like. They all called him Pops, because his hair and beard had patches of gray throughout. Ray had been twenty-nine years old the last time he was in County, not much older than most of these guys.

Ray listened as Bryan accepted the collect call.

"Hello, Mr. Stevenson!" Ray shouted. "I heard you wanted to talk to me, so here I am."

He smiled at a few of the guys who had looked his way when he yelled his greeting into the phone.

"Ray!" He could hear the excitement in Bryan's voice. "How are you doing?"

"I'm good." Ray had been discussing the case with Ben, one

of Bryan's staff attorneys. "Ben told me that Yates said he didn't see what he saw thirty years ago. I couldn't believe it, Bryan. Yates changed his opinion about the bullets. He was honest. It's a miracle."

"Ray, I have to tell you something. Yes, it's great news about Yates, but there's something else."

"What is it?"

"Well, Ray, I'm up here in New York City, in a hotel. You know I'm speaking at a couple of colleges. I was driving here, and I got a call from Judge Petro."

"Yeah?"

Bryan sounded breathless. "Ray, I had to have the guy pull over to the side of the road. She told me the district attorney had filed something electronically today. Without a word to anyone, they just filed a document electronically."

"What was it?" Ray asked.

"Ray, you're going home.

"They dropped all the charges against you.

"You're going home, my friend. You're finally going home."

Ray couldn't speak. He couldn't breathe. He couldn't think. He crouched down and sat on his heels. Then he leaned his back up against the wall and closed his eyes.

Home.

It had been so long since he'd heard those words.

Home. Ray was going home.

"Pops! Pops! You okay?" He opened his eyes, and the young thug was standing over him, concern on his face.

Ray smiled up at him and nodded.

"Bryan, this isn't no April Fools' joke, is it? You wouldn't do that to me, would you? It's April 1. That's not funny."

Bryan laughed. "It's no joke, Ray. The judge wanted to release you Monday, but I told her it had to be Friday. You are going to be released Friday morning. I'll be there, Ray. I'm not sure how I'm going to get there, but I will be there Friday morning at 9:30 a.m., and you and I are going to walk out of that jail, Ray. You're going to be a free man."

Ray laughed too. "I'll see you Friday, Bryan, and you'll bring me something to wear, won't you? I can't be walking out of this jail naked."

"We'll take care of it."

They were both quiet for another minute. There was so much to say; Ray couldn't find the words. Would he ever know how to thank this man? Bryan had been by his side for fifteen years and behind the scenes for even longer than that. Ray had gone to death row, and Bryan Stevenson had come there to bring him home. There were no words. There was no way Ray could repay him.

"God bless you," Ray said.

"Thank you, Ray." He sounded as choked up as Ray was, and they said their goodbyes. Ray hung up the phone, sat on the floor, and cried like a baby in front of all those gangsters.

He was going home.

Bryan was there Friday morning, and he brought Ray a nice black suit and a shirt that was the exact color of the Alabama sky. Ray changed out of his jail clothing and walked over to Bryan.

"How do I look?" he asked.

"You look good, Ray. You look good." Bryan had a suit on also, and a tie.

"We both look mighty fine. Is Lester here?"

"Yes, he's waiting for you outside. He's going to take you out of here, take you to his house. We'll give you a few days at home, but then I'd like to have you come down to EJI. There's a whole lot of my staff that have been waiting to meet you."

Ray nodded at Bryan. He was excited and nervous and just a bit overwhelmed. After so many years imagining this day, it was hard to believe he was going to walk out a door of his own free will.

"Ray, there's a lot of people out there. There's a lot of cameras and press. This is big news. I'm sure you've seen it. They want you to say a few words. Whatever you want to say, and if you don't want to say anything, then you don't have to."

Ray felt a flash of fear—and then he thought about the guys on the row. They would be watching the news. They would be seeing his release. Ray didn't know what he was going to say, but he would say something when the time came.

"Are you ready?"

"I'm ready."

He signed some papers for the jail and then walked to the double glass doors. Ray could see the crowd. He could see the cameras. He reached his hand for the door and then looked back over his shoulder at Bryan.

"You ready?" Bryan murmured.

"I've been ready for thirty years." Ray took a deep breath and walked out those doors with Bryan right behind him.

The crowd swarmed toward him. His sisters. His nieces. Ray could see Lester and Sia. He started hugging them all. His sisters were crying and praising God, and the cameras just kept *pop, pop, popping* at him. Ray reached out his hand to grab Lester's shoulder. Lester was in a pretty fancy suit himself.

It took a while for the crying and carrying on to die down. Everyone got silent, waiting for Ray to speak. He looked around at all the faces. He was a free man. There was no one who could tell him what to do or not to do. He was free.

Free.

He closed his eyes and lifted his face to the sky. He said a prayer for his mama. He thanked God. Ray opened his eyes and looked at the cameras. There had been so much darkness for so long. So many dark days and dark nights. But no more. He had lived in a place where the sun refused to shine. Not anymore. Not ever again.

"The sun does shine," Ray said, and then he looked at both Lester and Bryan—two men who had saved him—each in their own way. "The sun does shine," he said again.

And then the tears began to fall.

Ray climbed into Lester's car and buckled his seat belt. It was the first time he had been in the front seat of a vehicle in thirty years.

"Nice car," he said.

"It's old and tired. Like us." Lester laughed. "Where to?"

"I want to go to the cemetery. I want to see Mama's grave."

Lester pulled out onto the street and drove toward the highway.

"Take a right in two hundred feet," said a woman's voice.

Ray jumped in his seat. He whipped his head around to look in the back seat. He didn't see anybody. Where was she?

"Turn right," the voice said again.

"Where is she?" Ray whispered to Lester.

"Where is who?"

"The white woman in the car telling you which way to go?"

Lester looked at Ray blankly for a second and then started to laugh. He laughed for at least two miles. "It's GPS—the car's navigation system. There's no white woman hiding in the car, Ray, I promise you."

Ray realized that he had a lot to learn.

Ray looked at the gravestone with his mama's name. It made his heart hurt all over again. "I'm home, Mama. I told you I'd be home. Your baby's come home."

Lester stood next to him in silence as he cried for the third time that day. It was weird to be outside. No guards. No fences. Ray felt a weird kind of anxiety he'd never felt before. Lester must have sensed his uneasiness because he put his hand on Ray's shoulder and gave it a little squeeze.

They made one more stop before home—this time at a local restaurant with a buffet. Ray couldn't believe all the different choices. He loaded his tray with barbecue and biscuits and fried okra and banana pudding. He waited for his sweet tea while Lester walked in front of him. Lester stopped and handed a card to the cashier, and she handed it back to him. Without looking back at Ray, he kept walking toward a table.

Ray froze.

He didn't have any money. He hadn't seen Lester give the woman any money. Ray started to panic, and then he saw Lester turn around to look for him. Ray met Lester's eye and just stared at him while the cashier stared at Ray.

Lester walked back to Ray and whispered, "What's wrong, Ray?"

"I . . . I . . . don't have any money to pay her," Ray whispered back.

"I already paid her, Ray. Don't worry about it."

Ray could feel his chest pounding. Lester hadn't given her any money. He had been watching the whole time. Ray didn't understand what Lester was doing.

"Lester, I didn't see you give her any cash. I was looking the whole time. I'm not going back to jail for stealing some okra!"

"I paid with a debit card, Ray, not cash. It's okay. We're all paid up. You don't need to worry."

Ray followed Lester to the table and sat down. He could feel a lot of eyes on him. He knew he had been all over the news for days, since his release was announced. He hoped that was why people were staring. Ray hadn't used a fork in thirty years, so he fumbled with it and tried not to worry. *What if people are looking at me as the guy who got away with murder? What if they thought I really did it?* What if they said something? What would he say? Ray could feel the panic beginning again.

"Ray," Lester said quietly. "It's okay, Ray. Everything's okay. We're going to eat and then go home. You're going to sleep in a real bed tonight. It's all going to be okay."

Ray nodded. He wanted to get out of there. It was strange to be around so many people, to have his back to people. It made him uneasy.

He was free. He was really free. He was Anthony Ray Hinton. People called him Ray.

"Welcome home, Ray. Welcome home." Sia wrapped her arms around him, and Ray knew that before that day was done he was going to cry again.

They stayed up until close to 2:00 a.m. laughing and talking. They watched the late news and talked about how good Ray looked in his suit. When they finally said good night, Ray lay down in the guest room in the softest bed he had ever felt.

Ray knew on the row they would be just getting ready for breakfast. He could hear the sound of the guards walking up and down the tier. The clang of trays against each other. Men yelling good morning. The smell of sweat and grime. He could see and hear and smell it all.

It felt more familiar than the soft pillow under his head and sweet-smelling blankets that he had pulled up to his chin. It was all so strange, and he could feel the anxiety start again. Ray began to breathe heavy and fast. What was happening to him? Should he wake up Lester and have him take him to the hospital? Was this how it ended? The day he gets his freedom, he has a heart attack?

Ray tried to steady his breath, but it was like the walls were moving in and out and the room was spinning. He got out of bed and ran into the bathroom, locking the door behind him, Ray sat on the floor with his head between his knees, and immediately, his heart stopped pounding and his breathing slowed. He lifted his head and looked around. The bathroom was almost exactly the same size as his cell.

Ray stretched out on the bathroom floor, his head resting on the bath mat.

I'll sleep in here tonight. This feels like home.

Chapter Twenty-Six

BANG ON THE BARS

"Every night, I go outside and look up at the stars and moon, because for years I could not see either. I walk in the rain, because I didn't feel rain for years . . . I've never had an apology, but I forgave those involved in my conviction long before I left prison. I didn't forgive them so they can sleep well at night. I did it so I can."

—Anthony Ray Hinton[29]

Sometimes Ray tells people that he's the only man to get MVP in the NBA, the MLB, and the NFL. They look at him and some of them say out loud what all of them are thinking: *"You really lost it in there, didn't you?"*

Ray has spent the time since release telling his story to anyone who will listen. People from all walks of life want to hear his story now. He was asked to go to a private island and tell his story to a group of celebrities and others who are working hard to end the death penalty. Ray goes where he's asked to go—churches, colleges, small meeting rooms, private islands. He knows that he's a curiosity—the man who survived death row—but he also knows that he is a powerful voice for every man who still sits on the row. "I believe in justice," he tells crowds of people. "I'm not against punishment. But I don't believe in cruelty. I don't believe in useless punishment."

---

29 www.theguardian.com/lifeandstyle/2016/oct/21/28-years-on-death-row

One day at a church not too far away from Birmingham, a man raises his hand after Ray's done speaking and asks him what advice he would give to someone who found themselves in his position. "Pray," Ray says. "And when you're done praying, call Bryan Stevenson."

People always laugh when Ray says that. They laugh when he tells them about his marriages to Halle and Sandra and Kim. But laughing puts people at ease in a way that helps them to listen. It was true on death row, and it's true outside of death row.

And he needs people to listen.

Lester bought a house about two hundred yards from Ray's mama's house. Ray fixed up her house—and now he lives there by himself. He repaired the gazebo she loved so much. He still mows the grass the same as he did the day he was arrested.

People ask him how he can stay in Alabama. Why not leave? But Alabama is his home. Ray loves Alabama—the hot days in the summer and the thunderstorms in winter. He loves the smell of the air and the green of the woods. Alabama had always been God's country to Ray, and that did not change.

Ray loves Alabama, but he doesn't love the State of Alabama. Since his release, not one prosecutor, or state attorney general, or anyone having anything to do with his conviction has apologized. Ray doubts that they ever will.

He forgives them. Ray made a choice after those first difficult few weeks at Lester's when everything was new and strange and the world didn't seem to make sense. Ray chose to forgive. He chose to stay vigilant to any signs of anger or hate in his heart. They took thirty years of his life.

If he couldn't forgive, if he couldn't feel joy, that would be like giving them the rest of his life.

The rest of his life belonged to him. The State of Alabama took thirty years. That was enough.

It's been hard for Ray to get used to life outside of death row. Computers and the internet and Skype and cell phones and text messaging and email. He didn't know anything about all of that. A whole world of technology had happened while he was in his cell, and it wasn't easy to catch up. And as much as he tried to change it, his body and his mind still stick to the routines they learned on death row. Ray is up at 3:00 a.m. and ready for breakfast. Lunch is at 10:00. Dinner is at 2:00 p.m. He only sleeps on one corner of his giant king-size bed.

It's hard to create a new routine, but he tries.

Freedom is a funny thing. Ray has his freedom, but in some ways, he is still locked down on the row. He still knows what day they are serving fish for dinner. He knows when it's visiting day and at what point the guys are walking in the yard. His mind goes back there every single day—it was easier for his mind to leave the row when he was inside than it is now that he's free.

The first time he felt rain on his skin, he wept. He hadn't felt the rain in thirty years. Now when it rains, he rushes right into it. He'd never appreciated the beauty of rain until it was gone for thirty years.

For thirty years, the State of Alabama could tell him what to wear, when to eat, when to sleep, and they could take away his name and give him a number. They controlled every single moment of how he spent his life for thirty years. The one thing that belonged to him—that he had complete control of—was his own mind. His imagination. His perspective. His experience of reality. They couldn't lock up his mind. Or control it. Or threaten to kill it. His soul and his imagination were God-given and no one could touch those. In prison, how you do your time is how you live. You can fight and resist against every second of the clock and day on the calendar—or you can transcend time and space. Many couldn't understand it, but he was able to transcend time and space.

Without a doubt, Ray's imagination was the number one thing that helped him survive thirty years in hell. Staying sane on death row is hard enough—but it's a whole other thing when you know you are innocent. "When you are in a living, waking nightmare," says Ray, "you have to have a way to escape in your imagination." As far as Ray was concerned, the State of Alabama had kidnapped him and held him prisoner. He hadn't done anything wrong. He understands that he learned, as many trauma victims do, to purposefully disassociate himself from his experience. He's no psychologist—but he is a survivor.

Ray walks every morning, for as long as he wants and as far as he wants. He walks because he can walk. That also has a beauty he never saw before.

Ray carries scars that only Lester and Bryan see, and he only trusts them. He documents every day of his life. He always gets receipts. He purposely walks in front of security cameras. He doesn't stay home alone for too long without calling a few people to tell them what he's doing. He always calls someone to say good night. He's not lonely, or afraid to be alone. In many ways, he prefers to be alone.

He does it to create an alibi for every single day of his life because Ray lives in fear this could happen to him again.

A few days a week, Ray goes to Montgomery and works with Bryan and his staff at the Equal Justice Initiative (EJI). He travels around the country with Bryan or one of his staff and tells his story. Ray is over sixty, and he doesn't have any retirement income. He doesn't have the luxury of retiring, and he wouldn't even if he did. Retire from what? He had his retirement in his thirties and forties and fifties. Now, Anthony Ray Hinton is ready to live. He wakes up every morning grateful to be alive and grateful to be free. He speaks as a voice for the men still on the row. He is a voice for justice. He's the living image of all that is broken in our prison system.

He wants to end the death penalty. He knows firsthand that the justice system is a broken system. It's a barbaric system. It's not a system that elevates humanity. His faith tells him not to kill, and he never heard anything about that being conditional. The "monsters" on death row were once children who needed play and hope and love and stability just like anyone else. Many of them never got those things. Ray doesn't excuse their actions later in life, but he now believes, as Bryan Stevenson says, there is more to each person than the worst thing they have done. He does not believe anyone has a moral or a legal right to take a life—not even in exchange for another life. He believes that murder is wrong—even when you are the State and doing it for the people.

CRIME AND PUNISHMENT

"The more I know about the death penalty, the more problems I see with it. But what seems most pressing to me now is that the death penalty increases pain. It's like a machine that takes this terribly painful human event, and it takes that pain and replicates it and sends it spewing out in all directions."[30]

—Elizabeth Hambourger, Center for Death Penalty Litigation

"Capital punishment is the culmination of violence at both ends of society: the violence of the individual criminal, who is caught in a cycle of violence and whose life ends in a violent death; and the violence of the state, with its police forces and wars whose ultimate expression is the use of violent death as a form of retributive justice. In the middle, there is pain and sorrow for the families of the victims and of those who are sentenced to death, and for all the people with roles to play in the execution process. At the end of the day, capital punishment is a prison for the individual and society alike."[31]

—Mario Marazziti, 13 Ways of Looking at the Death Penalty

What about people who commit really serious crimes? What about when someone kills another human being? How do we hold them accountable? Doesn't the death penalty act as a deterrent, a warning against murder?

- Recent studies indicate that the American public is less inclined to support the death penalty when given

---

30 www.cjpcenter.org/poetic-justice-event-educates-regarding-the-death -penalty-but-also-heals-and-transforms/

31 www.yesmagazine.org/social-justice/2021/01/08/death-penalty-abolition -movement information about capital offenders, costs of execution, and alternative penalties.[32]

- States in the U.S. that do not employ the death penalty generally have lower murder rates than states that do. The same is true when the U.S. is compared to countries similar to it. The U.S., with the death penalty, has a higher murder rate than the countries of Europe, or Canada, which do not use the death penalty.[33]

Some believe that life in prison without parole, plus some form of restitution to victims' families, is an appropriate alternative to the death penalty. Others believe that life without parole involves the same injustices that exist with the use of capital punishment. "Life without parole has many of the same qualities that make the death penalty so abhorrent. Capital punishment is riddled with racial disparities, junk science, and a legal system that routinely fails the marginalized," making it "a punishment both extreme and one that disproportionately affects the most marginalized people . . . Thirty percent of lifers are 55 years of age or older, and nearly 4,000 inmates serving life were convicted of a drug-related offense; 8,600 people serving life with the possibility of parole or virtual life were sentenced as minors."[34] Some believe that long-term sentences with a focus on rehabilitation are the best thing for society.

32 www.ojp.gov/ncjrs/virtual-library/abstracts/instead-death-alternatives-capital-punishment

33 https://deathpenaltycurriculum.org/node/8?

34 www.motherjones.com/crime-justice/2021/03/are-life-sentences-a-merciful-alternative-to-the-death-penalty/

"Using the same mindset as killers to solve our problems demeans our own worth and dignity. Victims' families have every right initially to feelings of revenge. But the laws of our land should not be based on bloodthirsty, gut-level state-sanctioned killings: They should call us to higher moral principles more befitting our beloved victims."[35]

—Marietta Jaeger-Lane, whose daughter, Susie, was kidnapped and murdered by David Meirhoffer

Ray wants to make sure that what happened to him never happens to anyone else.

He wants to buy Lester an Escalade to pay him back for all the miles he put on his cars—for never missing a visiting day in thirty years. Looking forward to Lester's visits helped Ray mark and pass the time. The hours he spent with his best friend reminded Ray of who he was and where he was from and even where he belonged. Time with Lester had always been simple and easy and meaningful since they were boys. Having a constant presence of someone who believed in him helped Ray endure.

Lester wasn't an imaginary friend—he was flesh and blood and friendship and faith. His unwavering support steadied Ray. Year after year after year. He could never adequately put into words how Lester saved his life. Friendship can be even more powerful than family because the bond is built on time and

---

35 www.yesmagazine.org/issue/beyond-prisons/opinion/2011/05/28/the-night-i-forgave-my-daughters-killer

experience and a million different moments. Blood is blood, but friendship is a choice.

For Ray, there are so many things left to do in this world that he prays to God he will have the time to do them. He talks to his mom's picture every night and tells her that he's home. He cares for the place they called home, and he feels her presence every single day.

Every evening, he sits in the gazebo she loved. When there is an execution at Holman scheduled, Ray bangs his palm against the wood and murmurs the words he said fifty-four times before. "Hang in there. Don't give up. Hold your head high. We're here. You're not alone. It's going to be okay." Fifty-four times he never knew the right thing to say.

He still doesn't know.

Ray has lived a life knowing unconditional love. He learned on the row how rare that is. His mother loved him completely; so does Lester. His friendship with Lester is rare and precious, and every time Ray is invited somewhere to speak he brings Lester with him. It's the least he could do, and every once in a while, they look at each other and smile. It's wild. *Two poor boys from the old coal mining town of Praco, and they just shut down Buckingham Palace to give us a private tour.*

He got to see a Yankees game. He and Lester went to Hawaii. He gets asked all the time if he's gotten a girlfriend since his release and the answer is no—but he's open to dating and he's also still waiting for Sandra Bullock or Halle Berry or Kim Kardashian to give him a call.

Ray has kept busy, and he'd say he's been blessed. But he would trade it all to get his thirty years back, for just one more minute with his mother. He tries not to ask, "Why me?" He thinks that's a selfish question.

Why anyone?

McGregor passed away, and he wrote a book before he died. He mentions Ray in the book and says how evil Ray is, a clever killer that McGregor knew just from looking at him that he was guilty.

Ray forgives him. He figures someone taught him to be racist, just as someone taught Henry Hays. They are two sides of the same coin.

Ray forgives Reggie. He forgives Perhacs and Acker and Judge Garrett and every attorney general who fought to keep the truth from being revealed. He forgives the State of Alabama for being a bully. He forgives because if he didn't, he would only hurt himself.

He forgives because that's how his mother raised him. He forgives because he has a God who forgives.

Some days Ray is grateful to be free and determined to inspire and help, and other days he spends grieving what was lost.

Some things are easier to endure if you believe they will be over at any moment. If he could talk to young Ray now, he would tell his younger self that his mind is stronger than he knows. He would also tell him that someday he will share his story in a book, so write down everything he can so it's not so painful to relive later.

Stories matter. In getting to know the stories of others on death row, even the guards who managed his imprisonment and former Klan members like Henry Hays. Ray was always reminded that everyone has a story—every person makes choices, good and bad, and everyone has a reason for the choices they make. Innocent or guilty, every person's life matters. Every person's story matters. The books Ray read with his book club on death row made him feel not so alone, they helped him escape his own sad and unjust story through his imagination. They helped him write a new story for his life.

It's hard not to wrap your life in a neat and tidy story—a story that has a beginning, a middle, and an end. A story that has logic and purpose and a bigger reason for why things turned out the way they did. He would love to share his story with every single man and woman on death row in this country and every single person in prison around the world. His message to the men at Holman is the same as his message to everyone else—*Life is short. Forgive. Keep your faith in truth, in goodness, and in the ability of people to change. And hope is a light that can never be extinguished, no matter where you are.*

Ray looks for purpose in losing thirty years of his life. He tries to make meaning out of something so wrong and so senseless.

We all look for ways to recover after bad things happen. We try to make every ending be a happy ending.

Every single one of us wants to matter. We want our lives and our stories and the choices we made or didn't make to matter.

Death row taught Ray that it *all* matters. How we live matters.

As of April 2021, around 2,500 people are on death row in this country.

Statistically, one out of every ten people is innocent.

Each has a family, a story, a series of choices and events that have led to a life spent in a cage. Do you know who is wrongfully convicted? Do you know who is innocent?

Ray was once another name in a long list of names. Another person deemed irredeemable. The worst kind of cold-blooded killer that ever walked this earth.

Only it wasn't true.

Can we judge who deserves to live and who deserves to die? Do we have that right, and do we have that right when we know that we are often wrong? If one out of every ten planes crashed, we would stop all flights until we figured out what was broken. Our system is broken; isn't it time to put a stop to the death penalty? Bryan references the famous saying about how the moral arc of the universe bends toward justice, and he adds that justice needs help. Justice only happens when good people take a stand against injustice. The moral arc of the universe needs people to support it as it bends.

Do we choose love or do we choose hate? Do we help or do we harm?

Everyone can work for social justice and to create a judicial system that does not sentence you based on your income or your skin color. We can vote for politicians who believe that we have a system in need of reform and are willing to acknowledge the broken pieces and replace them. Ray believes that we need a system that gets to the root cause of criminality and leads with the belief that people can be rehabilitated and that every single life is worthwhile. "When men and women are exonerated and released from wrongful incarceration, they need support to transition back to noninstitutional life," Ray says. "They don't need cameras in their faces; they need help getting a driver's license, a job, and a safe place to live. They need help reintegrating into a quickly changing technological world. They need compensation for the years they lost. They need to know they are valued."

Who has value? How do you decide who matters?

"The death penalty is broken, and you are either part of the Death Squad or you are banging on the bars," Ray has said. "Choose."

And maybe some lives will change forever.

ACKNOWLEDGMENTS

First of all, I would like to thank my best friend, Lester. I've thanked him before and I will continue thanking him always. Since we were kids, he has stood by my side, and I have tried always to stand by his. I wish for everyone to have a friendship like ours, and since my release we have gone on to have just as many adventures as adults as we had as children.

I want to thank Bryan Stevenson and everyone at EJI. I was proud to be your client, and now I am proud to work alongside you fighting the good fight for justice. As I said before, you are a great lawyer, but you are also a great man and a great friend. I am blessed to have you in my life.

I would like to thank my literary agency for working just as hard on this middle grade book as they did on the adult version. Thank you, Doug Abrams. Thank you, Lara Love Hardin. I am grateful for you both.

I would like to thank the entire team at Feiwel & Friends for doing great books for children and young adults and for doing books that matter. Thank you to my editor, Kat Brzozowski, for having the vision to do a middle grade version and for knowing that young readers are hungry for stories and topics that matter. Thank you to the entire production and design and publicity team: Lelia Mander, Kim Waymer, Trisha Previte, Bonnie Cutler, Emily Heddleson, and Kelsey Marrujo.

I would like to thank especially Olugbemisola Rhuday-Perkovich for working so tirelessly to transform my story for young readers. This wouldn't be the book it is without you, Gbemi!

And finally I would like to thank all the young people who are reading this book, who I've gotten to visit in schools, who have heard my story and begun their important work to create a world that has more justice and equality for everyone. This book is for you, and I can't wait to see how each one of you changes the world.